The Definitive Step-by-Step Guide to Making Money on Airbnb

Evian Gutman

This book is dedicated to the Syrian refugees who forgo the basic human right to housing and shelter through no fault of their own.

Whilst just a small drop in the ocean, 10% of all book sales will go towards the **Unicef Syria Crisis Appeal.**

To learn more about this crisis and how you're able to personally make a difference, please visit:
www.unicef.org.au/appeals/syria-crisis-appeal

Contents

Preface

My Gran:	How's business?
Me:	Good granny.
My Gran:	That's good. Remind me again, what do you do?
Me:	Have you heard of *Airbnb*?
My Gran:	What is that?
Me:	You know the internet?
My Gran:	Yes. With computers?
Me:	Ummm, ye…
My Gran:	You sell computers?
Me:	No. I help people make more money renting out their homes on the internet
My Gran:	Where is the internet?
Me:	It's like, kinda everywhere.
My Gran:	And you use your law degree for this?
Me:	Not a whole lot.
My Gran:	So why are you doing this?
Me:	'Cause I enjoy it. And I'm pretty good at it too.
My Gran:	How do you have time to go everywhere? Will you be back for dinner?
Me:	Yes granny. I'll make sure I'm back for dinner.

Whilst my Gran, as adorable as she is, may not fall into the category of your "typical Airbnb host", her questions made me realize that many people are keen to understand why I now dedicate my time to helping Airbnb hosts get rich and successful, as well as why I'm an authority for helping them do so.

Where it all started...

I was living in New York; paying the equivalent of Switzerland's annual GDP in rent for a shoebox apartment that makes solitary confinement look like the Presidential Suite at the Shangri-La...

ABOVE: The kitchen / dining room / laundry of my 6th-floor walk-up. Monthly Rent: US$3,800

My roommate was dating a girl, who just like us, was paying waaayyyyy too much in return for waaayyyyy too little (*read*: she was living a standard New York life!)

Like many people in our situation, my first thought was *why am I stupid enough to keep living like this?!?*... followed shortly by... *and how do I subsidize this stupidity with a little extra coin?!?*

Enter Airbnb.

With the median home-sharing income for an Airbnb host in midtown Manhattan being a *not-insignificant* $8,286 per year, it becomes understandable why Airbnb has become the natural go-to solution for this commonly-held problem.

But whilst my roommate's partner was a lovely, intelligent and pretty girl who "ticked all the boxes"; her ability to describe her home and market herself on Airbnb was, well, simply not one of the boxes.

I'd spent the last few years gaining deep and broad marketing experience working in a variety of digital marketing roles both for professional service firms as well as freelancing for my own clients.

I was also a frequent, active and successful user of Airbnb myself.

I once covered my entire month's rent plus the cost of a two-week vacation to Mexico with the money I made renting out my place on Airbnb with a 10-day stay...

Upon leaving my previous employer, I was doing some freelance work providing digital marketing and copywriting services to small businesses.

Laughter at my roommate's girlfriend's Airbnb marketing failures quickly shifted to a realization that this background lined up perfectly with a niche sweet-spot of helping people to succeed on Airbnb.

It was in that moment that I realized my unique background and experiences lined up perfectly with helping new and existing Airbnb hosts overcome their commonly held challenges and frustrations with the home-sharing website.

Over the last few years, I've taken the time to transform my understanding of the Airbnb ecosystem from *power user* to *knowledgeable expert*. I've spoken with both hosts and guests across multiple continents to understand their goals, frustrations, successes and failures. I've helped hosts make thousands of dollars starting from a base of zero, and also saved guests bucket-loads with simple and practical Airbnb advice.

I've traveled between North America, Europe, Asia and Oceania to better understand various tourism markets and services; and invested in becoming an Airbnb thought leader that assists hosts the world over with best practice advice, tips, tools and resources - Check out my website **padlifter.com** and follow Padlifter on Facebook, Instagram and Twitter (**@padlifter**).

All of this started by simply helping Airbnb hosts optimize their listings and develop profit-maximizing pricing strategies. In the space of just over a year, Padlifter has grown to become the internet's go-to resource for Airbnb hosting tips and advice.

A prerequisite for overcoming the many hurdles and challenges that have presented themselves along that journey has been a genuine passion, interest and enjoyment in what I now do.

It's a great feeling to work with Airbnb hosts that are simply looking to make a bit of extra cash and have a little fun along the way. It's an even better feeling when almost all realize they've actually just made a ton of extra cash and had more fun than they ever thought possible doing something that was supposed to be "work".

I take pride in helping hosts make money on Airbnb and challenge their assumptions of what's actually possible and with what kind of commitment.

I'm excited to continue helping keen Airbnb hosts maximize their earning potential. This book is a small piece of that puzzle.

More times than not, all that's required to succeed on Airbnb is a gentle steer from someone that's been in the trenches themselves and earned their stripes.

Now if you'll excuse me, I've got dinner with my Gran…

How to Use This Book

Congratulations on taking the plunge in either becoming a new Airbnb host, or cementing the opportunities Airbnb affords if you're already an existing host.

Most Airbnb hosts possess a general understanding of the concept behind Airbnb: *Making money by opening up their home to travelers looking for short-term rental accommodation.* But Airbnb hosts, both new and old, frequently need to overcome a number of common challenges and frustrations:

New hosts are often...

- Not clear on what they need to do
- Finding Airbnb harder than it was made out to be
- Simply eager to get setup for success from the get-go

Existing hosts are often...

- Not making as much money as they would like to
- Not getting found often enough
- Struggling to convert listing views into booking requests

In this book, we address all of these concerns and cover the end-to-end hosting process to ensure you...

Get **found**
more often

Sell your
space

Maximize your
profitability

We will cover:

- Deciding if listing on Airbnb is right for you
- Getting your home ready to host
- Staying safe and protecting yourself and your property
- The step-by-step process for listing your place on Airbnb
- Building the perfect Airbnb listing that attracts reservation requests
- Developing a robust pricing strategy that maximizes your earning potential
- Being clever with booking and calendar settings to get found more often
- Knowing when to accept or decline guests and how to communicate with them appropriately
- Creating a seamless, enjoyable and efficient check-in process for both you and your guests
- Providing your guests with a phenomenal travel experience
- Cleaning and turning over your place with professionalism and efficiency
- Gaining 5-star reviews that win additional reservations
- Understanding payments and minimizing your tax obligations
- Working with co-hosts to get a little extra help with your listing
- The secrets of continual improvement

Regardless of whether you're an Airbnb newbie or long-time veteran, there's a lot to get right (and a lot you can get wrong!) This represents both a challenge and opportunity to you, for as they say... *the cream rises to the top*!

Get it right, and you'll join the exclusive club of Airbnb hosts that have leveraged this never-before opportunity for riches, fun and a true sense of belonging.

If you're a **new host**, it'll be a worthwhile use of your time to read this book cover-to-cover. We'll truly be going over the end-to-end process of hosting on Airbnb and everything that that entails. Reading through the entire book will guarantee you've dotted all your i's and crossed all your t's when it comes to learning how to succeed on Airbnb.

If you're an **existing host**, you're still encouraged to read through the entire book, but understand that you may already be familiar with a lot of the concepts and topics. Nonetheless, this book is more than just a "technical guide". All sections are peppered with tips, tricks, strategies and recommendations that will take you from good to great across all elements of the Airbnb hosting game.

And for **both** new and existing hosts – see this book as a permanent resource you're always able to reference for definitive answers to specific questions throughout your Airbnb hosting journey.

The book is set up into relevant chapters that makes it easy to parachute into the different elements of the hosting process and retrieve individual knowledge nuggets you're looking for at any point in time.

Remain keen and eager about the lessons you're about to learn. The best hosts combine their familiarity on the technical aspects of hosting on Airbnb with their passion, personality and zest for providing superior hospitality experiences. Through this formula, the lucrative financial rewards you receive shortly will be the inevitable product of your knowledge, energy and enthusiasm.

Have fun, enjoy the journey and become the incredible and successful Airbnb host you desire to become!

Deciding to List Your Place on Airbnb

What's the Opportunity?

Before embarking on your Airbnb journey, it's understandable that you want assurances that...

- The short-term rental property game is a **lucrative opportunity**
- **Airbnb** represents the best opening into that opportunity for you
- Your efforts and investments will translate into **riches and rewards** to your satisfaction

Here are some facts and figures that should validate the Airbnb opportunity and what you stand to personally gain...

An Idea Unlikely to Disappear any Time Soon

Since its inception in 2007, more than 60 million travelers have turned to Airbnb when looking for a place to stay.

Half a million people currently use Airbnb across 65,000 cities to put a roof over their heads each and every night.

More than 650,000 people across 191 countries have recognized this opportunity to monetize their extra space and showcase it to an audience of millions by becoming an Airbnb host.

Currently, there are more than 3 million listings on Airbnb. Airbnb accommodations account for 9% of total room inventory across all major U.S. cities. U.S. Airbnb hosts alone were responsible for generating $2.4 billion in just a single year, putting Airbnb's annualized revenue at about half that of the *entire* Hyatt Hotels group.

Throughout the summer of 2015, 17 million people used Airbnb to book a place to stay. And more guests traveled on Airbnb over that summer than the entire populations of Greece, Sweden or Switzerland.

20% of the 600,000 people who went to Brazil for the 2014 World Cup stayed in an Airbnb. 2.2 million tourists used Airbnb in 2015 to stay in the UK. And throughout Thanksgiving 2015, one quarter of a million Americans chose to stay in an Airbnb too.

But is it still growing? Absolutely! The total number of Airbnb guests have grown more than 600x in just five years. From 2013 to today, Airbnb has gone from 950,000 users to over 4 million in the U.S. alone. And within the U.S., the number of Airbnb homes almost doubled in Los Angeles, New York, San Francisco and Washington throughout 2015.

Summer travel on Airbnb has also grown 353x in just five years. And there has also been a 259% annual growth rate of people staying in Airbnb properties whilst on work trips throughout 2015.

Gain Additional Income

You're probably thinking… that's great for Airbnb, but what's in it for me? Well, if you're like the majority of other Airbnb hosts, then the primary motivation for listing your home on Airbnb is to gain an additional and lucrative source of income.

Over the past seven years, in the U.S. alone, Airbnb hosts have earned a cumulative $3.2 billion, of which the average Airbnb host individually makes $7,530 each year. On average, that's enough to offset…

- More than one year's worth of groceries
- 78% of mortgage repayments
- 10 months of transportation costs (including gas, vehicle expenses and insurance)
- One year's worth of a typical worker's contribution to family employer-provided health insurance (with $2,700 leftover!)

And how does this money meaningfully impact the day-to-day lives of regular people all around the world?

- For the average American family making $50,000 per year, that extra income is the equivalent of a 14% salary raise
- 53% of Airbnb hosts say that the money they make from hosting has helped them stay in their home
- 48% of an Airbnb host's income is used to pay for regular household expenses like rent and groceries
- 69% of Airbnb hosts in New Orleans use the money they earn on Airbnb to pay their rent or mortgage

How Much do You Stand to Make?

There's an entire chapter dedicated to pricing your place which will provide you with detailed insights into how much *you* personally stand to make by renting out your home on Airbnb.

But if Airbnb is something you're considering with any degree of seriousness, it'll be worthwhile doing some back-of-the-envelope calculations of your probable costs, likely revenue and potential profitability.

When it comes to **costs**, think about the "hosting essentials" you'll need to stock and furnish your place with. Some of these will be *one-off* costs associated with starting up your Airbnb such as furniture, bed linen and dinnerware. Others will be *recurring* costs such as rent, utilities and laundry.

When it comes to **revenue**, don't just think about how much you'll be charging for each night, but also how many nights you anticipate your place will likely be occupied (your "occupancy rate"). Will you have a weekend vs. weekday rate? Will you offer a weekly or monthly discount? Do you plan on charging a cleaning fee? All of these things will influence how much you stand to make and may also vary at different times of the year or by season too.

Social Benefits

Beyond the allure of making money on Airbnb, many hosts simply enjoy the opportunity of sharing their home with interesting people from all walks of life. Airbnb provides the opportunity for hosts to form connections with colorful personalities they would otherwise not have met.

Unlike hotel-stayers, Airbnb guests are not looking for "cookie cutter" accommodation options. Many guests are looking for more than just a roof over their heads – they're also looking for experiences and an opening into local cultures and communities too.

In fact, 85% of Airbnb guests claim that they choose to stay in an Airbnb so they can *live like a local...*

79% of Airbnb guests specifically want to explore a particular neighborhood (which are often outside the areas that hotels are commonly concentrated within). And as a side benefit, Airbnb guests choose to stay 2.1x longer in their destinations than non-Airbnb travelers.

All of this adds up to an opportunity for not only turning a decent profit, but also having some fun and meeting interesting people along the way too.

What Type of Airbnb Host do you Plan to Be?

People decide to enter the "Airbnb game" for a variety of different reasons...

Some are seeking a **consistent source of additional income** and decide to use Airbnb as their platform for doing so. Hosts like these may rent or buy a property with an additional room beyond their personal requirements with the intention of filling it as often as possible with Airbnb guests. These hosts may also be motivated by the social element of meeting new people they have the opportunity of sharing their home with too.

Other hosts use Airbnb in a more **sporadic and opportunistic way**. These hosts will rent out their homes on Airbnb whenever it makes sense to do so: They may put their place up for a couple of weeks while on vacation overseas. They may take in guests when out of town for a long weekend. Or they may permanently list their place and simply move into their partner's home whenever someone requests to book it.

Finally, there are hosts that approach Airbnb with a **true investment mentality**. These hosts will scout out a property for the specific purpose of putting it up on Airbnb. Their choice of property will be driven by whatever they believe will yield them the greatest rental income, and will then use Airbnb to seize that opportunity and maximize their full earning potential.

Knowing what type of host you wish to be is important.

It will influence how much time you invest in the "Airbnb game", the way you develop your pricing and marketing strategies, the guests you decide to accept or decline, and the likelihood of succeeding in hitting your individual goals and objectives.

Before diving headfirst into Airbnb, have a brief think about what *your* personal motivation for hosting is and what *you* would like to get out of it.

The Airbnb "Investor"

Not all short-term property rental markets are created equal. Some receive lots of travelers, whilst others receive far less. Some have high property costs or rent whilst others are much cheaper.

If your intention is to find a property for the specific purpose of making money on Airbnb, it'll be worth your while to hit the *pause* button momentarily and do some basic independent research before signing on the dotted line.

There are a number of tools out there to assist hosts in selecting investment properties optimized for making money on Airbnb.

You'll want to compare the rental performance, supply and demand of different properties in different markets; as well as understand the prices and occupancy rates those properties are able to command throughout different times of the year.

You may wish to check out Airdna's market summary reports, investment explorer and predictive pricing tools (**www.airdna.co**). These will help you gain competitive intelligence you'll want to consider when looking for an investment property or trying to optimize one you already own.

Investing without doing your due diligence or without being aided by data-rich insights to guide your decision-making process represents a naïve leap of faith and will rarely result in the most profitable outcome that's available to you.

Legality and Regulations to Consider

When deciding to become an Airbnb host, it's important for you to understand how the laws work in your city.

Some cities have laws that restrict your ability to host paying guests for short periods. These laws are often part of a city's zoning or administrative codes. In some cities, you're required to register, get a permit, or obtain a licence before you list your property or accept any guests.

Certain types of short-term reservations may be prohibited altogether. Local governments vary greatly in how they enforce these laws. Penalties may include fines or other enforcement.

City Regulations

Business Licences

Many cities and counties require owners or operators of certain businesses to apply for and obtain a licence before the business can be operated. Because Airbnb operations commonly resemble business activity, a business licence may in some instances apply. Many local governments have sections of their website explaining the business licensing process, and can provide you with relevant forms and information.

Who to Contact: Your city or county for more information

Building and Housing Standards

Most local governments and many states have rules and regulations that specify minimum construction, design, and maintenance standards for buildings. These include regulations on habitability, health, and safety. Certain rules applicable to residential and non-residential uses may be relevant to your listing. Some cities or counties may also require an inspection of your property to make sure it meets minimum habitability standards.

Who to Contact: Your local government to find out what standards apply to your listing

Zoning Rules

Most cities and counties have laws that set out the way you can use your home. These rules are often found in a zoning code, planning code, or city ordinances. You should consult these rules or regulations to see if your listing is consistent with current zoning requirements or use definitions.

Who to Contact: Your local government

Special Permits

Some cities or counties require a special permit to rent out your home.

Who to Contact: Your city or county government to see if you need one; and, if you do, how to get it

Taxes

Many cities, counties and states require hosts to collect a tax for each overnight stay; and to then pay that tax to the city or county. These may include things like hotel/transient occupancy taxes; sales, or other turnover taxes such as Value Added Tax (VAT), Goods and Services Tax (GST), or income tax.

Who to Contact: Your local government to see if you need to collect any taxes

Taxes are discussed in greater depth in the *Airbnb and Taxes* section on page 323. Airbnb also provide a list of city regulations that exist for many U.S. cities. If you are a U.S.-based Airbnb host, you'll want to take a look at Airbnb's *Responsible hosting in the United States* webpage (**www.airbnb.com/help/article/1376**), which covers city regulations that apply to many major U.S. cities.

Permissions

In addition to city regulations, you may also need permission to host your place on Airbnb from landlords, Homeowner's Associations, roommates and neighbors. Consider each of the following and get permission from any that are relevant to you before listing your place on Airbnb.

Contracts

Check your Homeowner's Association or co-op board regulations to make sure there is no prohibition against subletting your place, or any other restriction against short-term rentals. Ensure you understand your rights and entitlements under any leases, timeshare ownership rules, condo board or co-op rules, Homeowner's Association rules, or rules established by tenant organizations. Read your lease agreement and check with your landlord if applicable. You may consider adding a rider to your contract that addresses concerns and outlines the responsibilities and liabilities of all relevant parties.

Subsidized Housing

If you live in public, rent controlled, rent stabilized or subsidized housing; there may be special rules that apply to you. The manager of the property or your local Rent Board should be able to answer questions about this.

Roommates

If you have roommates, consider a roommate agreement in writing which outlines things like how often you plan to host, how you'll ensure guests follow house rules, and even whether you'll share revenue (if that makes sense for you).

Neighbors

Consider whether you should notify your neighbors about your plans to host, along with your plan for how to make sure your guests are not disruptive and remain respectful.

How to Have Difficult Conversations with Landlords

As just touched on, one of the challenges of hosting on Airbnb is simply getting the permission of landlords or Homeowner's Associations for putting your place up on Airbnb.

Whilst it is entirely possible to try host your place on Airbnb without having gained landlord permission, it is highly likely that it's only a matter of time till you get caught.

At best you've just damaged the trust and relationship you have with your landlord. At worst, you're in breach of contract, liable for damage, susceptible to getting evicted, and likely to lose security deposits or rent that you've already paid.

By default, the majority of landlords *will not* be supportive of your desire to put their place up on Airbnb.

The reasons for this are many and varied. As a relatively new concept, many landlords (especially older, less tech-savvy ones) will hold unfavorable perceptions of the "sharing economy" and short term rental platforms such as Airbnb. Other reasons include fears of property damage, being fined, voiding insurance policies, or additional inconvenience.

Before approaching your landlord, think about what their particular concerns are likely to be, and the recommendations you'll put before them to extinguish whatever concerns might be holding them back.

A lot of this will be circumstantial to the relationship you have with them, how long you've been in your place, what type of place it is, and the type of person you know your landlord to be.

Below are a few strategies for "winning over" your landlord. Not all of these ideas will be right for everyone, so think though your individual circumstances to determine which of these might work best for you...

Improvements in upkeep: Show your landlord other high-quality listings in your area that demonstrate that hosting on Airbnb would actually *increase* the cleanliness, care and upkeep of their place.

Financial security: Explain that hosting on Airbnb will provide supplementary income that will enable you to continue paying rent as well as encourage you to re-sign upon the end of the current lease.

Share in earnings: Offer to provide a share of earnings or undertake to self-fund minor renovations or home improvements that add value to their property.

Neutralize property damage and personal liability concerns: Share information on the *Airbnb Host Guarantee* and *Airbnb Host Protection Insurance Program* that provides protection against property damage and personal liability. Also offer to increase any security deposits currently held against you, or amend your existing contract to shoulder responsibility for certain types of damage.

Insurance policies: Offer to take out additional insurance policies that supplement any limitations of existing homeowner's, landlord or rental insurance policies.

Limitations on hosting: Agree to limit Airbnb rentals to bookings of specific trip purpose (e.g. no bachelor parties), to specific times of the year, or to conditional arrangements (e.g. whilst you too will be staying in the home). Remember to remain mindful of the Airbnb Non-discrimination Policy when doing so.

How Safe is Opening up Your Home to Strangers?

The idea of opening up your home to complete strangers naturally invites a number of legitimate concerns. Hosts will inevitably think about issues to do with safety, security, theft, property damage, cleanliness and lifestyle compatibility.

No opportunity to make a quick buck will justify anything that compromises your safety or security. You're also unlikely to accept Airbnb guests if you feel there's a risk of damage to your property or the potential of a personal liability claim being brought against you too.

Despite the pervasiveness of Airbnb, the prevalence of these issues tend to occur with minimal frequency. Long-time hosts inevitably have a story here or there of isolated incidents that murky an otherwise clean slate of positive hosting experiences. But by and large, Airbnb has proven itself to be a safe platform for short-term home renting.

Prudent hosts implement a range of preventative safeguards that maximize their safety and security to mitigate these risks and concerns:

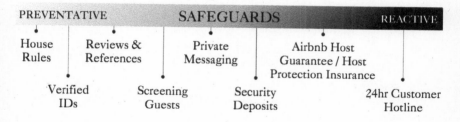

If you're excited by the opportunities afforded by Airbnb but still maintain safety and security apprehensions, then take the time to understand the range of measures available to hosts for mitigating the concerns you may currently hold.

Luckily, the ball is almost always in the host's court when it comes to taking charge of the 'who', 'what', 'where', 'when' and 'why' of hosting on Airbnb. There's also an entire chapter dedicated to *Safety, Security and Protecting Your Property*.

Getting Your Home Ready to Host

Create a Space That Will Appeal to Your Target Guests

Ideally, your Airbnb guests should enter your place and feel as if it's their own home-away-from-home. Just like hotels, doing so requires providing an ample standard of amenities, cleanliness, home furnishings and hospitality.

At the same time, guests choose to stay in an Airbnb *over* hotels for a reason: These travelers are frequently seeking something unique, special or different – things they're unlikely to find from a hotel (even a nice one!)

Remember that whilst your Airbnb activity may represent a dabble in the *property* game to you, it's completely different for your guests, who see Airbnb through a *hospitality* lens instead. Remaining aware of this important distinction will be crucial to creating a space that'll appeal to your guests and meet their expectations.

A critical part of furnishing your home is **understanding who your target guests are** and what kind of space they're likely to appreciate.

Are your typical guests retired elderly couples? Young travellers? Discerning business people?

Amadeus, a leading global tourism IT provider, have identified six distinct traveler "tribes" in a recent report:

Ethical Travelers:

Guided by ethical and/or environmental factors when organizing and undertaking their travel. An example is an environmentalist concerned about the carbon footprint and ecological impact of their travels.

Cultural Purists:

Treat their travel as an opportunity to break free from their typical home lives and immerse themselves in a different culture. An example is a traveler that learns a new language and the history of a country for an upcoming trip.

Obligation Meeters:

Have their travel choices restricted by the need to meet some "bounded objective". Examples include business travelers traveling for a conference, or a family traveling to attend a wedding.

Social Capital Seekers:

Influenced by their desire to impress friends and share travel experiences on social media. An example is a gap-year backpacker.

Reward Hunters:

Luxury travelers that seek indulgent "must-have" experiences. An example is a high-earning professional that is a member of a luxury travel club.

Simplicity Searchers:

Appreciate ease and transparency in their travel planning and holiday-making. An example is active seniors.

Make sure you pause to consider who your target guests are likely to be before deciding how you're going to furnish and decorate your home. Your guests will be more likely to enjoy their stay – resulting in better reviews, additional reservations and an easier job in managing each guest stay at your place.

Once you've determined who your target guests are, you'll need to think about how you're able to create a space that'll best accommodate them and their living preferences. Below are a few websites that'll provide you with a wealth of home décor and design inspiration:

Essentials for Your Home

Every home is different – be it the size, location or character. Nonetheless, there are essential items that every home listed on Airbnb should possess.

The following pages contain a list of items to consider stocking in your Airbnb. Some places simply won't need certain items (e.g. heaters in Hawaii) but the following represents a comprehensive list that should prevent your guests from ever saying "*I wish this place had a dot-dot-dot*".

For each item, you should strive to find something that satisfies the following **home furnishing purchasing principles**:

Price:
Given the sea of consumer options these days, why pay more for something you can get for less?

Functionality:
Does the item do what your guests would want, need and expect it to do?

Quality:
Spend the extra couple of bucks on buying items that elevate your home furnishings, amenities and hospitality standards.

Durability:
You're in the short-term home rental game. Make sure your purchases will withstand the test of time.

Replaceability:
Accidents inevitably happen. How easy / hard would it be to replace that one smashed plate?

Neutrality:
Your guests come in all shapes, colors and sizes. Pick unobjectionable items, colors and styles that are agreeable to most.

For the Entire Home

- Air freshener, potpourri or scented reed diffusers
- Air mattress
- Baby crib
- Broom and dustpan
- Doormat
- First aid kit
- High-speed Wi-Fi internet
- Magic eraser
- Mop and bucket
- Multi-purpose surface spray
- Phone charging cables
- Scrub sponges
- Toolkit
- Universal travel electrical adapters
- Vacuum cleaner
- Whiteboard

Bedrooms

- Alarm clock
- Bed
- Bed linen
- Bedside table
- Blackout curtains, shades or blinds
- Chest of drawers / dresser
- Duvet / comforter
- Duvet cover
- Extra blankets
- Ear plugs and eye masks
- Full-length mirror
- Good pillows
- Hangers
- Mattress
- Mattress protector
- Portable fan and heater
- Reading lamp
- Tissues (and tissue box cover)
- Throw pillows
- Wall clock

Bathrooms

- Bath mat
- Bath towels
- Body wash / shower gel
- Disposable razors
- Earbuds (Q-Tips)
- Full length mirror
- Hair dryer
- Hand soap
- Hand towels
- Hooks and towel racks
- Shampoo and conditioner
- Shaving cream
- Tissues
- Toilet brush
- Toilet paper
- Toilet plunger
- Toothbrush and toothpaste holder
- Toothpaste
- Trash Can

Dining Room

- Coasters
- Dining room chairs
- Dining room table
- Napkins
- Napkin holder
- Placemats

Laundry

- Clothes drying rack
- Dryer
- Iron
- Ironing board
- Laundry detergent and softener
- Laundry hamper
- Washing machine

Living Room

- Coasters
- Coffee table
- Lounge room chairs
- Media players
- Sofa
- Smart TV
- Streaming media services (e.g. Amazon Prime Instant Video, Hulu Plus, iTunes, Netflix)

Kitchen

- Aluminum foil
- Anti-bacterial surface cleaner spray
- Baking paper
- Can opener
- Coffee maker and coffee supplies
- Cutting boards
- Dinnerware set
- Dishwashing soap
- Disinfectant wipes
- Garbage bags
- Glassware set
- Hand soap
- Kettle
- Knife set
- Ladles
- Microwave
- Olive oil
- Paper towels
- Plastic cling wrap
- Pots and pans set
- Salt and pepper
- Serving spoons
- Silverware (cutlery) set
- Spice rack (and spices)
- Sugar
- Trash can
- Toaster
- Tongs
- Tupperware set

You can download the *Essentials for Your Home* checklist at **padlifter.com/home-essentials**.

Smart Homes

More and more homes are becoming "smart".

As defined on *Smart Home USA*, a smart home...

> *... is a residence that has appliances, lighting, heating, air conditioning, TVs, computers, entertainment audio & video systems, security, and camera systems that are capable of communicating with one another and can be controlled remotely by a time schedule, from any room in the home, as well as remotely from any location in the world by phone or internet.*

Whilst these items may not fall into the category of "home essentials", smart appliances are becoming increasingly standard expectations of young and discerning tech-savvy travelers. This category of travelers represents a large (and increasingly growing) share of Airbnb guests.

Smart appliances also provide benefits to the host. Owners of smart appliances are able to remotely manage and monitor key features of their home; such as electricity, security, heating and air-conditioning. In doing so, there are often associated cost savings achieved by being energy efficient and reducing electricity and water usage.

Below are a few smart appliances you may wish to consider adding to your place to take things up a notch...

Amazon Echo

- Capable of voice interaction, music playback, making to-do lists, setting alarms, streaming podcasts, playing audiobooks, and providing weather, traffic and other real time information
- Can control several smart devices using itself also as a home automation hub
- Plays music from Amazon Music, Spotify, Pandora, iHeartRadio, TuneIn, and more; using just your voice

Magiclight Bluetooth Smart Led Light Bulb

- Control a single bulb or group of bulbs
- Schedule your bulb to turn on or off at specific times
- Color options help change and elevate moods and decorative possibilities within your home

Nest Learning Thermostat

- An electronic, programmable, and self-learning Wi-Fi-enabled thermostat that optimizes heating and cooling of homes to conserve energy
- Learns people's schedule, at which temperature they are used to and when
- Uses built-in sensors and your phones' location to shift into energy saving mode when it realizes nobody is at home

Nest Protect Smoke and Carbon Monoxide Alarm

- Connect to Wi-Fi to receive an alert to your phone if the alarm goes off or the batteries run low
- Tells you "what" (smoke or carbon monoxide) and "where" so you know what to do
- Ability to "hush" alarm from your phone

Samsung SmartThings Appliance Hub

- Easily control, monitor, and secure your home from anywhere in the world
- Enables you to connect all of your different smart locks, lights, outlets, thermostats and more; and control them from the free *Samsung SmartThings* app
- Receive notifications about what's happening in and around your home and use your smartphone to remotely control your home's security, energy usage, lighting, and more

Samsung SmartThings Water Leak Sensor

- Get an immediate alert on your smartphone at the first sign of excess water
- Trigger a light or siren to turn on to alert if water is detected where it doesn't belong
- Prevent leaks from turning into floods

Wemo Switch

- Gives you control of your lamps and small appliances whenever you want and wherever you choose, with lots of options for scheduling and automation
- Plug in the Wemo Switch, download the free app, and control your lights and appliances from anywhere in the world, right from your phone
- No hub or subscription required

The **August Smart Lock** and **Schlage Keypad Deadbolt** are overviewed on page 253 in *The Check-In Process* chapter. Additional safety and security smart devices are also overviewed on page 64 in the *Safety, Security and Protecting Your Property* chapter.

Many smart appliances provide the ability to link the device with personal accounts you may hold on digital platforms (e.g. Amazon.com) or with service providers (e.g. Uber). Ensure that where this is the case, guests do not have the ability to use these devices to modify your account settings or utilize services that will be charged to you without your permission and/or consent.

Safety, Security and Protecting Your Property

Staying Safe

There is inevitably a small element of risk involved in opening up your home to an unknown guest. Naturally, this invites concerns around **safety and security** – both for yourself and your possessions.

Airbnb have a vested interest in ensuring that hosts feel safe and secure when putting their homes up on their platform. Anything that compromises their users' perceptions of safety or security represents the greatest threat to Airbnb's ongoing viability and success.

To address this, Airbnb have implemented a number of safeguards and mechanisms for mitigating these concerns. These are intended to provide peace of mind for its users.

Following a number of isolated incidents that garnered widespread negative media publicity, Airbnb developed a dedicated *Trust and Safety Team*. Today the team number more than 250 full-time staff, who are available around-the-clock in every time zone.

In the event that you ever need to contact them, Airbnb hosts can reach the Customer Support hotline for emergencies by dialing **(+1) 855-424-7262** or their local number equivalent (*see next page*). Store these numbers in your mobile phone and keep them handy in other easy-to-access places too.

Argentina: +54 1153 527 888

Australia: +61 2 8520 3333

Austria: +43 720 883 800

Brazil: +55 21 3958 5800

Chile: +56 229 380 777

China: +86 10 5904 5310

Denmark: +45 8988 2000

France: +33 1 8488 4000

Germany: +49 3030 8083 80

Greece: +30 211 1989 888

Hong Kong: +852 5808 8888

Ireland: +353 1 697 1831

Israel: +972 3 939 9977

Italy: +39 06 9936 6533

Japan: +81 3 4580 0999

Mexico: +52 55 4170 4333

Netherlands: +31 20 5222 333

New Zealand: +64 4 4880 888

Norway: +47 2161 1688

Peru: +51 1 708 9777

Poland: +48 22 30 72 000

Portugal: +351 30 880 3888

Puerto Rico: +1 787 919 0880

Russia: +7 495 465 8090

South Korea: +82 2 6022 2499

Spain: +34 91 1234 567

Sweden: +46 844 68 1234

Switzerland: +41 4350 84 900

UK: +44 203 318 1111

U.S.: +1 415 800 5959

To speak with a Customer Support team member, you will need to call from your verified Airbnb phone number, or alternatively provide that number at the beginning of the call.

The average wait time is less than 15 minutes, and the hotline caters to a variety of different languages.

Obviously, the best outcome is addressing problems or concerns before they escalate.

You're also able to send an email to the Customer Support team to seek guidance or advice for non-emergency issues that still relate to your safety and security. To do so, visit: **www.airbnb.com/help/contact_us**.

This is what you will see:

Safety concerns

In an emergency situation, or if someone's been injured, contact local police or emergency services immediately

Step 1
Call local police or emergency services

911
Your local emergency number

Step 2
Once you're safe, report the issue to us

Email us
Connect with our Trust & Safety team

Tell us what's going on

Including detailed info will help us get you to the right person

Send email

Alternatively (and again only if the issue is not an emergency), Airbnb hosts can also direct message the Airbnb Customer Support team on Twitter using the handle **@AirbnbHelp**. A team member will usually respond within a matter of minutes, and if the issue can't be resolved easily, will often be escalated so you receive an email or phone call to discuss further.

As Airbnb state, in the event of an emergency, make sure to contact your local police or emergency services immediately and before contacting Airbnb.

Property Damage and the $1M Airbnb Host Guarantee

According to Airbnb, they're committed to creating a safe and trusted community, and understand that hosts may at times need protection.

To achieve this, they've created the **Airbnb Host Guarantee**, which they claim will reimburse eligible hosts up to $1M for damage to possessions or property caused by Airbnb guests.

Airbnb espouse the claim that your peace of mind is priceless, and will therefore protect your property for every booking at no additional cost to you. Airbnb further hail the Host Guarantee as representing an unmatched level of protection against damage to personal property within the travel industry.

Airbnb stipulate that there are still limitations to this protection. In some instances there will be *limited* protections for things like jewellery, collectables and artwork.

In other instances, there will be *no* protections at all for things like cash and securities, pets, personal liability, or possessions housed in shared and common areas.

Keep this in mind when deciding **what you choose to store in your place** and **where you choose to store it.**

The jury is still out on just how reliable the Airbnb Host Guarantee actually is in providing the protection hosts are looking for when it comes to addressing property damage to their place.

In the absence of that certainty, you should also consider additional ways you're able to protect your property. These include using your **common sense**, requiring Airbnb guests to provide **security deposits**, taking out **additional insurance policies** and installing **safety and security equipment** within your home. All of these are discussed in greater detail towards the end of this chapter.

These additional protections should represent your "first lines of defense" when it comes to avoiding property damage or when trying to receive compensation. The Airbnb Host Guarantee can then help you sleep easy at night knowing you have a back-up plan should all else fail.

Obtaining any payout from the Host Guarantee will be conditional on meeting strict procedural requirements (*outlined shortly*) for submitting a claim. Failure to meet these requirements through even minor missteps, may prevent making a successful claim.

You're therefore strongly encouraged to take a moment to familiarize yourself with the Host Guarantee *now* (or at a time prior to needing to make a claim).

In the event that you need to submit a claim, go to: **www.airbnb.com/incidents/new**. Once you select an eligible booking, Airbnb will ask you the following questions:

- Date that the damage was discovered
- What has been done to date to resolve the concern
- What happened, and who was involved
- A description of the damage
- Estimation of the value of damage
- How you would like the claim resolved

Hosts also have the opportunity to upload supporting documentation, such as photos and police reports.

Submission of a Host Guarantee payment request is conditional on the host certifying that:

- They agree to Airbnb's Approved Payment Request Agreement
- The information and materials they have submitted are true and complete
- They have complied with the Airbnb Host Guarantee Terms and Conditions and Terms of Service
- They understand that Airbnb may prosecute any false or fraudulent activity in connection with the Airbnb Host Guarantee to the full extent of the law

Approved Payment Request Agreement	As set forth in the Airbnb Host Guarantee Terms and Conditions, completion of this payment request requires your agreement to the Approved Payment Request Agreement.
Certification	☐
	By checking this box, I agree that my typed signature below be accepted as my written signature and hereby certify and attest that, to the best of my knowledge, all of the above information and submitted materials are true and complete and I have complied with the Airbnb Host Guarantee Terms and Conditions and Airbnb Terms of Sevice in connection with this submission. I understand that Airbnb may prosecute any false or fraudulent activity in connection with the Airbnb Host Guarantee to the full extent of the law.
Full name	

Back   Submit

The Case Against

Despite its claimed protections, the Host Guarantee is not without its critics who say that it may not actually deliver, when push comes to shove.

Critics claim that it provides a false sense of security to Airbnb hosts and that the protections afforded by the Host Guarantee are ad-hoc at best or unreliable at worst. The main criticisms are that it...

- Only provides protection for *excess* coverage
- Will be void if you fail to adhere to strict claim submission process requirements
- May also be voided if you fail to adhere to local laws

We'll take a look into each of these criticisms below, and run through the things you need to know about each to maximize your level of protection.

Only Providing Protection for Excess Coverage

A gray area of the Host Guarantee is whether Airbnb have the ability to "pass the buck" before they're obliged to consider a claim that's brought before them.

The Airbnb Host Guarantee Terms and Conditions include the following two clauses:

> You acknowledge and agree that any amount of Covered Losses payable to you under the Airbnb Host Guarantee **will be reduced by the amounts you have already collected for the same Covered Losses from a source other than the Airbnb Host Guarantee**, including without limitation: (i) amounts received under an insurance policy, guarantee or indemnity; (ii) a security deposit; or (iii) payment directly by the Responsible Guest or an Invitee, or other party or an insurer or guarantor of such party.

> These Airbnb Host Guarantee Terms are **not intended to constitute an offer to insure, do not constitute insurance or an insurance contract, and do not take the place of insurance obtained or obtainable by you.**

Are hosts therefore expected to also possess additional insurance policies? Are hosts obliged to have first exhausted all other avenues before making a claim under the Host Guarantee? And are existing insurance policies considered *primary protection*, with the Airbnb Host Guarantee to be considered only *excess* coverage?

The answers are regrettably not entirely clear. But here is what we do know...

Airbnb have made verbal assurances that they frequently provide compensation under the Host Guarantee prior to hosts having exhausted other existing insurance policies. Despite these claims, anecdotal stories from frustrated Airbnb hosts and the opinions of insurance professionals suggest that this has not and will not be common practice.

And whilst Airbnb may simply represent a bit of extra pocket money for you, your little home-sharing operation may, legally-speaking, be considered a *commercial endeavour* for the purposes of tax and the law.

Because of this, many homeowner's insurance policies will reject claims arising from damage caused from an Airbnb booking. These policies may consider a short-term Airbnb rental to be a commercial operation that requires its own distinct commercial insurance (just like a hotel) – not homeowner's insurance.

Despite all of this, the Airbnb Host Guarantee still places an obligation on Airbnb to payout a claim – even if that requires having exhausted all other avenues of coverage first. Therefore, so long as all other means – insurance policies, security deposits, guest payments and the like – have been exhausted, the Host Guarantee should, theoretically, kick in.

Failure to Adhere to Strict Claim Submission Process Requirements

The process for submitting a claim under the Host Guarantee is incredibly rigid and strict.

Here is a summary of the process for submitting a claim under the Host Guarantee:

1. **Contact Guest**

   Contact guest to notify them of the complaint. Attempt to negotiate a resolution.

   No resolution?

2. **Determine Eligibility**

   Review Airbnb's Host Guarantee Terms and Conditions. Determine if you have an eligible claim.

   Is there an eligible claim?

3. **File Police Report**

   Filing a police report is a requirement for payment requests that exceed US$300. It is also still encouraged for all other requests too.

   Police report filed?

4. **Compile Documentation**

   Useful documentation and information will help process payment requests ASAP. This includes:
   - Proof of damage in the form of photographs or videos
   - A filed police report (with report number, name of officer, and phone number)
   - Receipts or some alternative evidence of the accurate fair market value or report cost.
     - For *property*, provide original purchase price, date purchased, and current condition
     - For *fixtures and furnishings*, provide the estimated cost of repair or replacement
     - For *artwork*, provide original receipts or other proof of original cost
   - Proof of ownership in the form of receipts, photographs or videos
   - Any other documentation you feel will be helpful for processing your request

   Documentation compiled?

5. Submit Request to Airbnb

Send Host Guarantee submissions to Airbnb within 14 days from the guest's check out or before the next guest checks-in – whichever is earlier.

Submitted within 14 days or before next guest checked-in?

6. Airbnb Follow-Up

Within 24 hours, Airbnb will send you a confirmation email and follow-up emails to discuss next steps (such as further documentation they require).

Sent all additional documentation requested by Airbnb?

7. Airbnb Notification of Outcome

Upon receipt of sufficient information from both the host and the guest, Airbnb will review all documentation, evaluate the payment request, and contact the host upon completion. The length of the process will vary depending on the severity of the case, the quality of documentation, and the cooperation of the host and guest. Airbnb strive to resolve most cases within a week of submission.

As you can see, making a claim is no walk in the park. Airbnb oblige hosts to have performed specific (often complicated and time-consuming) actions within onerous timeframes to be able to claim under the Host Guarantee.

As an example, is it feasible to have a tradesman come in and provide an estimated cost of repair or obtain a police report before your next guest check-in (which may be that same day or tomorrow)? To be eligible to make a claim under the Host Guarantee, an Airbnb host would have needed to have done that!

If seeking to make a claim under the Host Guarantee, become familiar with all requirements of the policy to ensure that your claim is not denied simply on procedural grounds. The best way of doing this is understanding these requirements *before* a time you need to rely on them.

Failure to Adhere to Local Laws

It's no secret that many people are technically operating their Airbnb listings in contravention to local laws.

These are often relatively minor contraventions, be they the number of days their place is rented out each year, through to a failure to collect local taxes.

Be mindful that if operating your Airbnb in violation of any zoning or other local laws, Airbnb may reserve the right to deny a claim under the Host Guarantee.

Legality and regulations to consider are covered on page 30 of the *Deciding to List Your Place on Airbnb* chapter.

Protecting Your Property

Whilst the Airbnb Host Guarantee may have its limitations, you are not limited in the ways you are still able to add additional independent protections for your property yourself. There are a number of options you have for doing so. These include:

- Using **common sense**
- Adding a **security deposit** to your Airbnb listing
- Taking out **additional insurance policies**
- Installing **safety and security equipment** within your home

Each of these are overviewed below.

Common Sense

It may seem obvious, but the easiest way to prevent property damage is to use your common sense and remove valuable possessions that are likely to get damaged from your place.

Whilst you don't want to sterilize your place in a way that rids it of personality or prestige, small steps can go a long way in minimizing the risk of needing to rely on things like the Host Guarantee or security deposits.

A few simple things you may want to consider doing include:

- Removing or locking-up any valuables from your home and the places that guests have access to
- Replacing expensive or valuable items with cheaper alternatives of lesser concern if damaged or broken (e.g. silverware, dinnerware sets and furniture)
- Being selective when screening guests to identify "high-risk" booking requests more likely to cause damage (e.g. bachelor party groups)

Security Deposits

Whilst the Airbnb Host Guarantee is designed to protect against rare instances of damage, a security deposit can be useful for smaller, simpler accidents that occur during a reservation – like a broken glass. Security deposits are often the quickest and easiest way of avoiding the headache of filing claims with your insurer or trying to meet the strict procedural requirements of the Airbnb Host Guarantee.

If a host wants to make a claim on the security deposit, they must do so within 48 hours of the check-out date. If a claim is made, Airbnb will mediate and collect payment from the guest, as necessary. Security deposit amounts must be between $100 and $5,000 USD.

Before adding a security deposit, be conscious that adding too large a security deposit (or one at all) may be a potential disincentive for some guests considering which place they want to book. Whilst security deposits are fairly common features of Airbnb listings these days, make sure that it isn't the reason a prospective guest decides not to book your place.

When deciding how much to charge, hosts are advised to research comparable listings in their local area and see how much other hosts are charging for *their* security deposits. This will give you a feel for how much you may wish to charge for *your* security deposit and the extent to which security deposits are being used generally.

Your security deposit will only apply to reservations made after you've added it to your listing – it won't retroactively apply to existing reservations. Security deposits also can't be handled off-site in cash. Off-site payments are a violation of Airbnb's Terms of Service.

To add or edit a security deposit:
1. Login to Airbnb
2. In **Hosting** mode, select **Listings** from the top navigation bar
3. Select **Manage listing** for your listing
4. Click **Pricing** from the menu at the top
5. Click the **Edit** button for the **Extra charges** section
6. Enter an amount between $100 and $5,000 USD into the **Security deposit** input box
7. Click the **Save** button

Extra charges

Cleaning fee
This fee will apply to every reservation.

$

Security deposit
If you submit a damage claim within 14 days of checkout, guests will be responsible for damages up to this amount.

$

Extra guests
After more than: 1 guest, charge $0 per person, per night.

$

For each guest after

1 ⌄

Weekend pricing
This nightly price will replace your base price for every Friday and Saturday.

$

Save   Cancel

Taking out Additional Insurance Policies

For true peace of mind, prudent Airbnb hosts should take out additional insurance policies.

Typically, these include **individual home and contents** insurance policies**, rental** insurance policies and **landlord** insurance policies. Some of the more comprehensive policies combine these into a single, standalone policy.

These policies provide a range of protections that often include protections for and against:

- Your liability to a guest or other person
- Damage to property
- Loss of rental income
- Temporary accommodation
- Identity theft
- Valuable items
- Losses exceeding $1 million
- Damages from indirect causes
- Damages from delays

Many insurance policies have *exclusion* or *limitation* clauses that restrict protections or limit your ability to make claims. Because of the unique (and still largely ambiguous) legal status of short-term rental properties and rental arrangements like Airbnb, many "standard" protections are frequently not covered under traditional policies. Hosts often discover this only after the fact when seeking to make a claim.

Ensure that any additional insurance policies you take out do not include a *business activity exclusion clause*. Furthermore, ensure that your Airbnb activity does not legally constitute business activity if this will void any of the protections. Similarly, existing landlord insurance policies may not cover your Airbnb rental for the same reasons. Ensure you check that this is not the case for your policy.

Some new policies designed specifically for short-term rentals such as Airbnb allow you to get single, short-term policies that provide coverage for only the nights that you have confirmed reservations. This flexibility is useful for hosts that tend to primarily take only sporadic or ad-hoc reservations.

For hosts that more frequently or consistently book out their space on Airbnb, many of these insurance companies also offer longer-term cover in the form of 6 or 12 month policies (and often with a discount).

For maximum protection, find a policy that protects against liability, building and contents as well as lost business income.

Adding Safety and Security Equipment

Safety Equipment

You may wish to install safety equipment within your home. This includes things like smoke detectors, carbon monoxide detectors, first aid kits, fire extinguishers and locks on bedroom doors.

Beyond the heightened level of safety and security you gain, one additional benefit is enabling you to then list any of those items as "safety amenities" on your Airbnb listing for guests to see.

Some guests search for properties that specifically have these safety amenities. This means that listings that don't have them won't show up in search results for those searching guests.

Adding safety equipment therefore provides a simple, yet useful way of differentiating yourself from other listings on Airbnb.

Security Equipment

In addition to protecting your home and guests from accidents and emergencies, you may also wish to install security equipment to prevent and inform you of malicious guest activity.

There are a range of "smart home" monitoring services that will centrally monitor your home as well as alert you with instant notifications via text or email in the event that a potential safety or security issue requires your attention.

You're able to install sensors that can monitor windows, doors and items of importance. These sensors will notify you about potential security concerns or malicious activity. For example, you may wish to be notified if a door is opened excessively over a short period of time or find out if your valuable items are being touched or compromised.

Below are examples of security equipment you may wish to install at your place:

Nest Cam

- When Nest Cam detects activity, it can send a phone alert or email with a photo of the event
- Built-in speaker and microphone allows you to talk and listen through the app
- Ability to get a special alert if a person is seen, and will then save 10 or 30 days of continuous video history to the cloud

Nest Cam Outdoor Security Camera

- When Nest Cam Outdoor Security Camera detects activity, it can send a phone alert or email with a photo of the event
- Weatherproof camera, cable and adapter; so you can leave it out in the rain
- Built-in speaker and microphone allows you to talk and listen through the app

Scout Wireless Window and Door Sensor and Alarm

- Triggered when a window or door opens or closes
- Receive custom alerts, or enable custom responses based on the activity
- Great for monitoring sensitive areas such as jewelry safes and liquor cabinets

Legality, Notification and Consent

It's important to remember that good hosts respect their guests' privacy.

You *must* notify your guests about any security cameras or other surveillance devices that you've installed in or around your home and get consent where required.

The use of surveillance equipment may also be against the law in some places, so make sure you understand any applicable laws first.

Protecting Against Personal Liability

Airbnb offer the **Host Protection Insurance Program** to protect Airbnb hosts (and landlords, as additional insureds) against liability claims of up to USD 1 million that occur in a listing or on an Airbnb property during a stay.

The Host Protection Insurance Program provides primary liability coverage for up to $1,000,000 per occurrence in the event of a third-party claim of bodily injury or property damage related to an Airbnb stay.

Airbnb claim that this Program can serve as your primary coverage for eligible claims filed as a result of Airbnb stays – even if you already have existing homeowner's or renter's insurance. The Program will only act as the primary insurance coverage for incidents related to an Airbnb stay, but is available to hosts regardless of other insurance arrangements they may or may not already have.

You do not need to do anything to be covered under the program – by agreeing (or continuing) to list your property on Airbnb, you automatically agree to be covered under the program for occurrences during Airbnb stays (subject to Airbnb's policy terms). Program coverage is subject to a $1,000,000 cap per listing location, and certain conditions, limitations, and exclusions may apply.

It also covers landlords and Homeowner's Associations in many cases when claims are brought against them because a guest suffers bodily injury during a stay, and may also cover claims if a guest damages building property. This often includes claims filed by a landlord against a host. Landlords are covered only if Airbnb and/or the host are also a party to the claim.

The Airbnb Host Protection Insurance Program is different to the Airbnb Host Guarantee. The former is designed to protect hosts against third party claims by guests of *bodily injury or property damage*, whereas the latter is designed to protect hosts against damage to their *property and possessions* in the instance of damage caused by guests staying at their place.

The Host Protection Insurance Program does not apply to liability arising from:

- Intentional acts of assault and battery, sexual abuse or molestation (by the host or any other insured party)
- Loss of earnings
- Personal and advertising injury
- Fungi or bacteria
- Chinese Drywall
- Communicable diseases
- Acts of terrorism
- Product liability
- Pollution
- Asbestos, lead or silica

Examples of What's Covered

- A guest breaks their wrist after slipping on the rug and brings a claim for the injury against the host.
- A guest is working out on the treadmill in the gym of the apartment building. The treadmill breaks and the guest is injured when they fall off. They bring a claim for the injury against the host and the landlord.
- A guest accidentally drops their suitcase on a third party's foot in the building lobby. The third party brings a claim for the injury against the host and the landlord of the host's building.

Examples of What's Not Covered

- Intentional acts where liability isn't the result of an accident
- Accusations of slander or defamation of character
- Property issues (e.g. mould, bed bugs, asbestos, pollution)
- Auto accidents (e.g. vehicle collisions)

Who Does it Apply to?

The Host Protection Insurance Program is currently available for hosts in:

Australia · Austria · Belgium · Canada · China · Croatia
Czech Republic · Finland · France · Germany · Hungary · India
Ireland · Israel · Italy · Japan · The Netherlands · New Zealand
Norway · Portugal · Singapore · Spain · South Africa · Sweden
United Kingdom · United States

To file a claim under the Host Protection Insurance Program, contact
Airbnb at **www.airbnb.com/contact** and Airbnb will route you to their
third party claims administrator.

Screening Guests

The ball is still in a host's court as to whether or not they wish to host a prospective guest. **Hosts can decline any reservation request they feel uncomfortable with.**

When doing do, hosts have the option of choosing whether or not they wish to provide a reason for why they've chosen to decline the request.

As a word of caution however, declining many or most reservation requests can negatively impact your placement in search results.

When deciding whether or not to accept a reservation request, use all information available to you to determine whether it's a booking you wish to accommodate. Below we outline some of the key things you should consider when screening guests to decide if you wish to host them:

- Verified IDs
- Reviews and references
- Your own further independent research

Despite having the ability to screen guests and decline reservation requests, Airbnb hosts should remain mindful of Airbnb's Non-discrimination Policy and its principles of inclusion and respect.

The policy outlines rules around accepting or declining reservation requests as well as stipulating a prohibition against indicating a preference for guests of a particular race, color, ethnicity, national origin, religion, sexual orientation, gender identity or marital status.

When first listing your place on Airbnb, you'll be required to accept the following:

I agree to treat everyone in the Airbnb community – regardless of their race, religion, national origin, ethnicity, disability, sex, gender identity, sexual orientation, or age – with respect, and without judgement or bias.

Accept   Decline

Breaches of the policy may result in a range of measures being taken against hosts; such as an insistence to remove language that's in contravention to the policy, confirming explicit intent to comply with the policy or suspension of accounts. Be sure to familiarize yourself with this policy before you screen guests and decide who you do and do not let into your space.

Verified IDs

Airbnb users have the opportunity of verifying their identity by connecting their Airbnb profiles to other social networks as well as scanning official ID and confirming personal details. These users earn a verified ID badge on their profiles:

Guests with multiple forms of verified ID provide a higher threshold of authentication that enhance their trustworthiness and credibility.

These guests will have provided a Passport or Drivers Licence; linked their social media accounts (each of which requires its own additional forms of verification) and have confirmed a real email address and phone number to Airbnb.

Verified info		Connected accounts	
Government ID	✓	Facebook	✓
Personal info	✓	Google	✓
Email address	✓	LinkedIn	✓
Phone number	✓		

All of this should help in building a more complete picture of who you're actually dealing with.

Despite this safeguard, anyone attempting sly or malicious behavior on Airbnb may still be able to do so. The Airbnb ID verification process is not foolproof, and even Airbnb state that it is not an endorsement or guarantee of a guest's identity.

In theory, there is nothing stopping someone from making fake accounts or finding ways to cheat the verification processes if that were their objective. These forms of added verification therefore need to be understood within that context.

For prospective guests that lack multiple forms of verified identification, consider asking additional or more probing questions to gain the assurances that would otherwise have been forthcoming had they provided them.

Ways in which *hosts too* are able to use the Airbnb verification process to demonstrate credibility is covered on page 288 in the *Building Trust and Getting 5-Star Reviews* chapter.

Reviews and References

Hosts are also able to look at a prospective guest's reviews and references prior to accepting a reservation request.

Hosts can trust that any review they see on a guest's profile is the result of the guest having actually stayed at another Airbnb host's place. Reading prior host reviews will be the best insight into the type of person a prospective guest is likely to be. A large number of positive reviews should also reinforce this.

Despite the rigorous review process, many Airbnb hosts end up giving better reviews to their guests than they may deserve. This occurs for a number of reasons. Psychology suggests that human nature is biased towards keeping unflattering thoughts to oneself unless there's a strong reason for doing otherwise. Many hosts also (wrongfully) fear "retribution" reviews they believe they will receive if giving a bad review to a guest (see the *Leaving Reviews* section on page 307 for more information on this). And some hosts also leave no review simply out of laziness or forgetfulness.

Therefore take a "big-picture" perspective when trying to get a feel for a prospective guest based on their reviews. Ninety-nine *glowing* reviews with one less-than-shiny review is better than five standalone *averagely-good* reviews. Humans are still humans.

For less-than-glowing reviews, try to understand the crux of the issue: Was it specific to the individual reservation, or is there a consistent pattern of negative behaviors to be concerned about? Was there a particular disagreement between host and guest, or does the review flag an ongoing safety concern?

Trying to understand the nature of any issues will help in predicting the likelihood of their recurrence or anything you might need to consider when deciding whether or not to accept a reservation request.

Also distinguish reviews that simply *aren't bad* from those that are *actually good.* The former shed little light on the type of person the prospective guest truly is, and at best indicate that no noteworthy issues arose on a given host's watch. The latter are true testimonials to the good character of the guest and frequently provide insight into why that is so.

A host that takes the time to spell out each and every little thing that made the guest as great as they're being made out to be is going above and beyond what the review process requires of them. This is a personal choice. You can therefore take a lot more comfort and place more value on reviews of this nature.

References, though much easier to obtain and influence, are also handy insights into a prospective guest's good character.

Reviews and references are covered in greater detail in the *Building Trust and Getting 5-Star Reviews* chapter on page 287.

Your Own Further Independent Research

Where possible, use identifying information you've been able to ascertain yourself to conduct your own further research.

Even though you will only have limited information to work off, Airbnb profiles may just provide you with little nuggets of information that you're then able to utilize to dig a little deeper.

Some Airbnb users will list the school or university they went to as well as the place that they work. If you're lucky enough to receive a reservation request from someone with a unique name or other specific identifying information; using all of this to do a quick search on Google, Facebook or LinkedIn may provide a wealth of information.

Listing Your Space on Airbnb

Less Daunting than You May Have Thought...

Listing your space on Airbnb may feel like a daunting decision, and one surrounded by uncertainty for first time hosts.

Fortunately, the process is surprisingly simple, and Airbnb break it down into three "compartmentalized" steps:

1. Starting with the basics
2. Setting the scene
3. Getting ready for guests

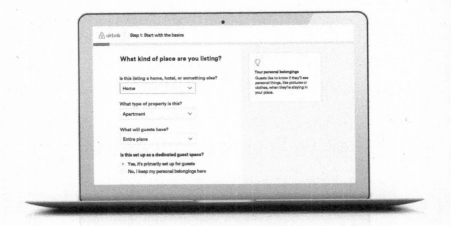

Within each step, Airbnb guide you through a set of questions that enable you to customize what you're offering and the types of bookings you'd like to receive.

The following pages contain a run-through of the end-to-end process for getting your listing live on Airbnb...

Step 1: Starting With the Basics

It's important to remember that guests searching on Airbnb filter their searches to find a space that best match their needs.

Some of the basic search filters they're able to specify include location, travel dates, room type, guest numbers, price range, Instant Book, number of bedrooms, beds and bathrooms, Superhost status, amenities, house rules, neighborhoods, facilities and host language:

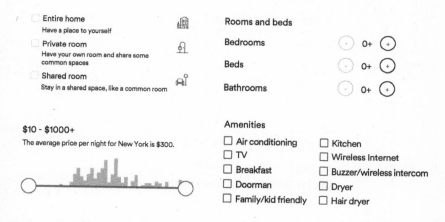

Therefore, when initially setting up your listing, Airbnb will require some basic information so that your place is able to get found in search results by guests looking for what you have to offer.

Below are all of the things you'll need to tell Airbnb, to develop a comprehensive listing that'll help guests find your place and satisfy what it is they're looking for.

A. What Kind of Place are you Listing?

You begin by telling Airbnb...

What kind of place are you listing?

Is this listing a home, hotel, or something else?

Home	⌄

What type of property is this?

Apartment	⌄

What will guests have?

Entire place	⌄

Is this set up as a dedicated guest space?

○ Yes, it's just set up for guests
○ No, I keep my personal belongings here

For your typical host, this is most commonly an apartment or house. Other common property types include bungalows, cabins, condominiums, guesthouses, in-law apartments, guest suites, townhouses and holiday homes. It even includes options as wacky and obscure as treehouses, lighthouses and castles.

You then tell Airbnb whether your place is a home, hotel or something else; and then specify how much space guests will have exclusive access to. Your options are:

1. The **entire place** – Guests will exclusively rent your entire home (this includes in-law units)
2. A **private room** – Guests share some spaces but they'll have their own private room for sleeping
3. A **shared room** – Guests won't have a room to themselves

You'll also tell Airbnb whether it's setup as a dedicated space for guests or whether you keep your personal belongings there too.

B. How Many Guests can Your Place Accommodate?

Your next step will be to tell Airbnb:

- How many **guests** your place can accommodate
- How many **bedrooms** guests can use; and
- How many **beds** guests can use

C. What Kind of Beds Does Your Place Have?

You have the option of specifying **bed details**, which help guests understand what the sleeping arrangements are like.

Based on how many bedrooms and beds you previously indicated guests can use, Airbnb will enable you to specify the bed details for each of those rooms, as well as for any common spaces too.

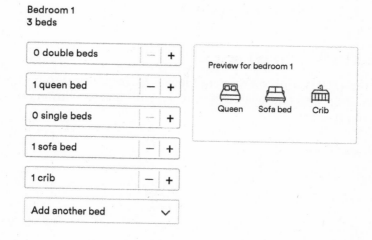

D. How Many Bathrooms?

You'll then tell Airbnb **how many bathrooms** your place has.

If you're listing your place as a private or shared room, you will also specify whether the bathroom is private or shared. If you have a toilet separate from the shower, you count it as a 0.5 bathroom.

How many bathrooms?

Bathrooms (−) 2 (+)

Are any of the bathrooms private?

○ Yes

○ No, they're shared

E. Where's Your Place Located?

You'll then tell Airbnb **where your place is located** by entering your full address. Your exact address will only ever be shared with guests *after* a confirmed reservation.

Where's your place located?

Country

United States ▾

Street Address

100 3rd Avenue

Unit / Apartment / Suite / Building (optional)

Apartment 10

Suburb / Town   State

New York   NY

Post Code

10003

100 3rd Avenue Apartment 10, New York, NY 10003, United States

Edit address

Drag pin to change location.

Once your listing goes live, you'll also be able to specify **location amenities**. These include:

- Beachfront
- Lake access
- Ski in / Ski out
- Waterfront

F. What Amenities do you Offer?

You'll then tell Airbnb **what amenities you offer**. Whilst none are required, providing these will help guests feel at home in your place and add a nice touch to make them feel welcome and comfortable.

The amenities you're able to specify as offering include:

- Essentials (towels, bed sheets, soap and toilet paper)
- Wi-Fi
- Shampoo
- Closet / drawers
- TV
- Heat
- Air conditioning
- Breakfast, coffee, tea
- Desk / workspace
- Fireplace
- Iron
- Hair dryer
- Pets in the house
- Private entrance

You're also able to specify any **safety amenities** you offer. These include:

- Smoke and carbon monoxide detectors
- First aid kits
- Safety cards
- Fire extinguishers
- A safety card
- Locks on bedroom doors

Once your listing goes live, you'll also be able to specify a whole range of **additional amenities** too. These include:

- Kitchen amenities (e.g. microwaves, coffee maker, dishes and silverware, and cooking basics)
- Facilities (e.g. free parking on premises, gyms, pools and spas)
- Outdoor space (e.g. BBQ grill, patios, balconies, gardens and backyards)
- Special amenities (e.g. breakfast and beach essentials)
- Family amenities (e.g. baby bath, changing tables and cribs)

Also once your listing is live, you're able to specify **accessibility** features, such as:

- Step-free access to your home
- Path to entrance being lit at night
- Wide hallway clearances and doorways
- Lifts in the building
- Flat smooth pathways to front door
- Disabled parking spots
- Accessible-height beds and toilets
- Firm mattresses
- Grab-rails for shower and toilet

To specify these additional amenities and accessibility features (as well as other home safety and location features) once your listing is live:

1. Login to Airbnb
2. In **Hosting** mode, select **Listings** from the top navigation bar
3. Select **Manage listing** for your listing
4. Click on **Listing details** from the menu at the top
5. Click the **Edit** button for the **Amenities** section
6. Click the **Edit** button for the **Additional**, **Family**, **Logistics**, **Accessibility**, **Home Safety** or **Location** sections
7. Select all relevant amenities, logistics and accessibility, home safety and/or location features that are applicable to your place
8. Click the **Save** button

G. What Spaces can Guests Use?

You'll then be required to specify the **spaces guests can use**. These are spaces on *your* property. Your options include:

- Private living room
- Pool
- Kitchen
- Laundry – washer
- Laundry – dryer
- Parking
- Lift
- Hot tub
- Gym

Don't include laundromats or nearby places that aren't part of your property. If it's okay with your neighbors, you can include a pool, hot tub, or other shared space.

Step 2: Setting the Scene

In this next step, you'll help paint a picture for prospective guests to understand your space and all the reasons they would want to book it. You'll be asked to upload photos and provide descriptions of the different spaces you have on offer or any other selling points for your place.

A. Show Travellers What Your Space Looks Like

Airbnb will ask you to upload photos of your place.

Including photos of all the spaces a guest can use will help prospective guests imagine what a stay at your place would be like.

You can start with just one photo and come back later to add more. Alternatively, you can skip adding photos altogether till after you complete the rest of the listing process.

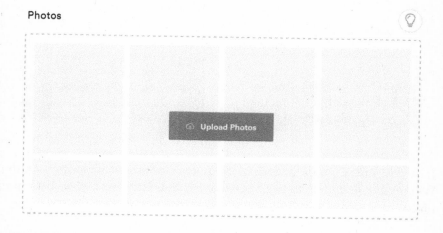

Your first photo will be the photo that gets displayed for your listing in search results, as well as the photo displayed at the top of your listing page.

The following page illustrates an example of this.

SEARCH RESULTS   **LISTING PAGE**

It is typically a photo of either the master bedroom or lounge room. Whatever you decide to use, make sure that it showcases the best your place has to offer.

If you plan on taking photos yourself, you'll want to get your hands on some high-quality but affordable photography equipment such as a DSLR camera, electronic flash, tripod and wide-angle lens.

Photos are covered in greater detail on page 106 in the *Building the Perfect Listing* chapter.

B. Edit Your Description

Once you've uploaded a photo (or a few), Airbnb will ask you to provide a little more information to help in setting the scene. To begin, it will ask you for a **listing summary**, which is a brief overview of your place that guests read before they get into the details. You only have 500 characters to write your summary.

The information you provide for your listing summary will appear at the top of your listing page and answer common questions guests have when looking for a place to stay.

Creating a best-practice listing summary is covered on page 117 in the *Building the Perfect Listing* chapter.

You can specify here if your place is good for families (with kids), big groups and/or pets.

You'll also be given the opportunity to elaborate on the different elements of your listing. These include:

- **About Your Place:** An overview of the key selling points of your place
- **What Guests Can Access:** An overview of the spaces that guests will have access to within your home
- **Your Interaction with Guests:** Information on how you'll be available to offer help and/or socialize throughout the stay
- **Other Things to Note:** Other details that may impact a guest's stay (for better or worse)
- **About the Neighborhood:** Information on what makes your local area great or unique and any key local attractions
- **How to Get Around:** Information on public transport, driving and walking options

Completion of any of these additional descriptions is optional, and Airbnb state that only 30% of hosts add more information here. You are nonetheless strongly encouraged to take the time to complete these descriptions. The additional investment of your time here will pay its dividends with a best-of-class listing that helps you stand out from the crowd and receive additional bookings.

Creating a best-practice Airbnb listing is covered on page 114 in the *Building the Perfect Listing* chapter.

C. Name Your Place

You'll need to come up with a **listing name** which is a very brief title for your listing. You only have 50 characters to work with and Airbnb will provide examples of other listing titles nearby.

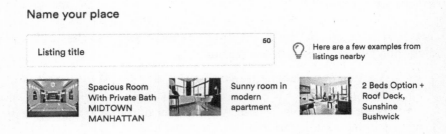

How to create a best-practice listing name is covered on page 116 in the *Building the Perfect Listing* chapter.

Step 3: Getting Ready for Guests

A. Manage Your Guests Requirements

Before your listing goes live, Airbnb like to ensure that hosts feel confident about every guest that arrives at their place. That's why they require certain information from all guests before they're able to book.

You begin by reviewing the Airbnb requirements that all guests must meet before they can book:

- A profile photo
- A confirmed email address
- A confirmed phone number
- Payment information
- Agreement to your house rules
- Send you a message about their trip purpose
- Confirm their check-in time if arriving within 2 days

New guests must also acknowledge that each place is unique, that they will respect their host's place, and that they will stay in touch with their host.

You also have the option of adding both/either of the following additional requirements:

- Government-issued ID submitted to Airbnb
- Recommendations by other hosts and having no negative reviews (new Airbnb guests who haven't yet been reviewed will always need to send you a request to book)

These optional settings are intended to provide hosts with comfort and certainty around who they let into their homes and space. Keep in mind that if you require another host's recommendation, first-time Airbnb guests won't be able to book instantly, which may mean fewer bookings.

B. Set Your House Rules

Only guests who agree to your house rules can book. Here you can let guests know if their trip is a right fit for your home.

Airbnb provide some recommendations on common house rules. These include specifying whether:

- Your place is suitable for children (2-12 years)
- Your place is suitable for infants (under 2 years)
- Your place is suitable for pets
- Smoking is allowed
- Events or parties are allowed

You also have the option of adding any rules of your own too, such as quiet hours or no shoes in the house. In the rare event a guest breaks your house rules, you can cancel online 100% penalty-free (i.e. no fees, no blocked dates, no loss of Superhost status).

House rules are covered in greater detail on page 126 in the *Building the Perfect Listing* chapter.

You are also provided with the opportunity of telling Airbnb any **details guests must know about your home** here. These include:

- Must climb stairs
- Potential for noise (and when it's likely to take place)
- Pet(s) live on property
- No parking on property
- Some spaces are shared
- Amenity limitations (e.g. weak Wi-Fi or limited hot water)

C. Successful Hosting Starts With an Accurate Calendar

Airbnb remind you that guests will be able to book available days, so you should keep your calendar up to date to avoid surprise reservations. They also remind you that if you cancel because your calendar is inaccurate, you'll receive penalties and those dates will be blocked.

All that's required here is ticking a check-box that says *"Got it! I'll keep my calendar up to date."*

D. Getting Started With a Couple of Questions...

Airbnb will ask you a few simple questions to help customize your calendar settings.

The first question Airbnb will ask you is **have you rented out your place before?** You can choose between:

- I'm new to this
- I have

The second question Airbnb will ask you is **how often do you want to have guests?** You can choose between:

- Not sure yet
- Part-time
- As often as possible

E. Set Limits on Trip Length

You have the option of deciding how long guests can stay by setting a minimum and maximum trip length:

By default, there is no minimum or maximum trip length. Shorter trips can mean more bookings, but will require you to turnover your space more often.

It's recommend that new hosts do not implement a minimum stay requirement when starting off on Airbnb. This will help build up your number of bookings as quickly as possible.

Minimum stay requirements are covered on page 172 in the *Booking Settings, Calendar Management and Getting Found* chapter.

F. Choose How Much Notice Guests Must Provide

You're required to specify how much advance notice you would like before a booking. Your options are:

At least *one day*'s notice can help you plan for a guest's arrival, but you might miss out on last-minute trips. If you choose *Same Day*, you also specify the exact hour that guests must book before.

You can also specify when guests must **check-in** by specifying a check-in window that includes a "From" time (8am on the day of the booking till 1am on the day following the booking) and a "To" time (9am on the day of the booking till 2am on the day following the booking). You also have the option of making either (or both) ends of the check-in window flexible.

G. Choose How Far Out Guests Can Book

You're able to specify how far in advance a guest can book. Your options are:

- All future dates
- 12 Months into future
- 6 Months into future
- 3 Months into future
- Dates unavailable by default

H. Do you Want to Sync Your Airbnb Calendar With Another Calendar?

Here you have the option of automatically syncing your Airbnb calendar with other calendars that you may already be using to rent out your property. If you list your space on other websites, this prevents multiple guests from booking the same dates.

Your external calendar options include:

- Google Calendar
- HomeAway
- iCloud
- VRBO

Instructions for importing your external calendars is covered in greater detail on page 176 in the *Booking Settings, Calendar Management and Getting Found* chapter.

I. Update Your Calendar

When your listing goes live, guests will see your calendar and be able to book available days. Here you're able to look over your monthly calendars and pre-block any days you already know you do not want to make your place available for bookings.

<	>	February 2017					Block all dates

Mon	Tue	Wed	Thu	Fri	Sat	Sun
		1	2	3	4	5
6	7	8	9	10	11	12
13	14	15	16	17	18	19
20	21	22	23	24	25	26
27	28					

J. How do you Want to Set Your Price?

You have 2 options for deciding how you want to set your price:

1. **Price adapts to demand:** You set a base price and price range. You tell Airbnb's Smart Pricing tool to automatically adjust your price based on your settings.
2. **Price is fixed:** You set a base price. Airbnb gives you price tips that you can accept or ignore.

Airbnb state that the "right price" can change as the number of searches for listings like yours goes up and down. They therefore recommend setting your price to adapt to demand. This is the default option unless you choose to fix your price.

Regardless of whichever pricing option you choose, you'll still continue to get price tips from Airbnb to help you set prices for your listing.

If you Choose 'Price Adapts to Demand'...

You'll be required to select a price range, with your price automatically adjusting within the range that you set. When there are fewer searches for listings like yours, a lower minimum price will be offered, which will help you get bookings.

Smart Pricing

Select a price range
Set your price to automatically adjust within the range you set.

Minimum

$50 per night

Tip: $54 · Set ⑦

Maximum

$220 per night

Tip: $230 · Set ⑦

You're also required to set a **default nightly price**, which should reflect the space, amenities, and hospitality that you provide.

This base price is the price guests will see for reservations that are more than four months away (since Airbnb will provide a "dynamic" nightly price only for the upcoming next four months). Also, if you choose to turn Smart Pricing off, your nightly price will default to this figure.

When setting your base price, Airbnb will offer you a price tip which you're able to accept or overwrite with your own default nightly price. The amount that Airbnb recommends is based on your listing's qualities, nearby prices and demand. Price tip amounts increase for most hosts after the first booking.

Here you will also specify your relevant currency.

If you Choose 'Price is Fixed'...

Here too you are still required to specify a base nightly price and currency for your nightly rate. And here too, Airbnb will also offer a price tip which you're able to accept or overwrite with your own figure.

You can always change your default nightly price at a later time in response to changes in demand.

For example, a higher price may help you earn more during busy travel seasons, while a lower price may get you more reservations when travel is slow.

Many hosts choose to start off with a lower default nightly price and raise it after earning a number of positive reviews. This helps them attract guests that may otherwise overlook them in preference for more established listings that may be perceived as more reliable or desirable.

Edits you make to your default nightly price will only apply to reservations booked after you make the changes. Changes do not apply to upcoming reservations that you have already accepted.

Determining your optimal nightly price is covered in greater detail on page 145 in the *Pricing Your Place* chapter.

K. Kickstart Your New Listing With a Welcome Offer

Airbnb provide you with the ability to give travelers extra reason to be the first to stay in your home by offering a 15% discount to your first guest. New listings that get booked and reviewed in the first month appear more often in search results and get an average of 3.6x more bookings in their first 3 months.

Airbnb will share your offer with some guests who've searched in your area. Dozens of people will see your home, but only one person will be able to claim the offer. Your first guest can use the offer to book any time in the next three months. If no booking is made, you can cancel the offer by editing your calendar. Otherwise, it will automatically expire after one month.

If you do not activate the welcome offer during setup, you will no longer be able to add a special welcome offer once you finish publishing your listing.

L. Discounts

To encourage longer stays, some hosts set a **weekly** or **monthly discount.**

If you want your listing to appear in searches for reservations of 28 nights or more, you'll need to set a monthly discount. Weekly discounts will apply to any reservation of 7 - 27 nights.

Airbnb will offer a weekly and monthly discount price tip which you're able to accept or overwrite with your own amounts.

Discounts for longer-term stays are covered in greater detail on page 162 in the *Pricing Your Place* chapter.

M. Review Your Settings

You will then review the settings you have just specified for your place, which includes:

- Your guest requirements
- Your house rules
- Availability
- Pricing

Upon review, you have the ability to go back and edit any of these should you wish.

N. Summary of What to Expect Once You Publish

Airbnb will summarize what you can expect once you publish your listing.

Update your calendar

Keep your calendar up to date so guests only book when you're able to host.

Refine your controls

Guests who meet your requirements can book a trip instantly. Everyone else will send you a request to book.

Receive bookings

You'll immediately get a confirmation email with information like why they're coming, when they're arriving, and who they're coming with.

You have the ability to go back and edit your calendar, guest and booking requirements.

Airbnb also remind you of your protections, such as 24/7 customer support, the $1M Host Guarantee, and penalty-free cancellations for reservations you feel uncomfortable with.

note that for **receiving bookings** you have two options
w you will allow guests to book your place:

ly: You allow guests to book instantly without needing
onsent to their reservation request

2. **quest:** You will review and respond to each individual
reservation request after deciding whether you wish to accept
or decline it

By default, this is set to *Instantly*. If you wish to require all guests to
book *by request*, Airbnb will require you to confirm that you
understand...

1. You'll only have 24 hours to respond to requests without penalty
2. Your listing will be ranked lower in search, so you may get
fewer reservations
3. You'll lose some host protection and controls, including penalty-
free cancellations for reservations you're uncomfortable with

Airbnb remind hosts that guests prefer to book instantly and that over
600,000 hosts let guests book instantly because they can get up to
double the bookings with less work.

Airbnb's Instant Book feature is covered in greater detail on page 193 in
the *Booking Settings, Calendar Management and Getting Found* chapter.

O. Your Local Laws and Taxes

As a final step, Airbnb will ensure that you've familiarized yourself with
your local laws, as well as their Non-discrimination Policy.

Depending on your listing's location, Airbnb may provide some general
information on things such as local laws, taxes, rent regulation, zoning
codes and business licences. Airbnb encourage hosts to consult a local
lawyer or tax professional if they are unsure of anything.

Building the Perfect Listing

Understanding Your Target Guests

Before diving head-first into building the perfect Airbnb listing, it's important to first take a step back to consider who it is you are trying to attract to come stay at your place.

Why? Because Airbnb is active in 65,000 cities and 191 countries. With more than half a million Airbnb stays each night, there are a lot of guests out there looking for a place to stay. All too often, Airbnb hosts make the mistake of casting their net as wide as possible in the hope of appealing to anyone that happens to stumble across their listing.

The reality however, is that in attempting to be *everything-to-everybody*, they often end up often becoming *nothing-to-nobody*.

The Airbnb hosts that ultimately receive the most reservation requests are those that understand what *type* of Airbnb guest is most likely to be interested in their place and then "positioning" their listing to directly appeal to *those* target guests.

Will they inevitably lose possible bookings? Potentially.

Will these losses be offset by the vast increase in bookings from a smaller number of keener target guests? Most likely.

And will these target guests have a better experience being hosted in a way more aligned to their travel needs and preferences? Almost certainly!

Remember our different guest types you may want to consider targeting...

Ethical Travelers	Cultural Purists	Obligation Meeters
Social Capital Seekers	Reward Hunters	Simplicity Searchers

Understanding who your target guests are and then tailoring your Airbnb listing to appeal specifically towards them will increase the number of reservation requests you receive.

These reservations will also arrive from guests more likely to enjoy their stay and leave positive reviews. As a virtuous cycle, all of this will lead to additional bookings from similarly-interested target guests in the future too.

Ensure that as you bulk up and build out your Airbnb listing, you remain mindful of who it is you're trying to attract at all points in time.

Starting With a Trustworthy Profile

It wasn't long ago that the idea of opening up your home to complete strangers from all around the world was an idea that would be dismissed as silly at best or dangerous at worst.

Airbnb now not only compete head-to-head with traditional travel accommodation options like hotels, but look likely to overtake them in popularity and usage too. A critical foundation of this success is the comfort felt by guests towards Airbnb that overcome trust, safety and security concerns.

Both hosts and guests need to feel absolutely confident that each other are trustworthy, reliable and pose no threat or safety concern. The importance of establishing trust, credibility and rapport with prospective guests is a prerequisite for any hope of success on Airbnb.

The easiest and most effective way to create trust and rapport is with an Airbnb profile that provides a window into who you are, why you're great, and helping prospective guests imagine how these qualities will translate into a phenomenal travel experience.

Whether your goal is to receive more listing views, additional reservation requests or simply to make more money – the critical dependency common to each is the necessity for guests to first feel comfortable that their host is trustworthy, reliable and likable. Without this, your place has a much lower chance of being considered by guests when deciding where they might want to stay.

In few other places on Airbnb is it easier for hosts to have a profound impact on their likelihood of success than by developing a likeable and trustworthy **Airbnb profile.**

Your profile may end up being the decisive factor that tips prospective guests sitting on the fence towards booking your place over others they're also considering.

The following is an overview of all the different elements of an Airbnb profile and how you're able to utilize each for maximum effect.

Profile Description

Compare the following two Airbnb profile descriptions:

Hey, I'm Thomas!
New York, New York, United States · Joined in March 2010

I'm from Los Angeles. I moved to New York for work. I'm 33 years old, any my favorite thing to do is hang out with my friends.

VS.

Hey, I'm Thomas!
New York, New York, United States · Joined in March 2010

Hi there,

I'm Thomas. I'm a 33-year old guy originally from sunny California, and whilst I miss my friends and family back home (not to mention the beach!), I absolutely love my new home here in NY!

By day, I'm a Creative Director at an advertising agency, and by night I'm an ice-cream enthusiast, comedy aficionado and lover of Broadway shows.

I enjoy traveling the world and creating new experiences. My favorite countries are Argentina, Croatia, India and Australia. Through these travels, I've been fortunate to learn what a good Airbnb experience (and host) looks like: A great home, with a friendly host, in an awesome neighborhood, and the ability to do the things you love! I try ensure that each and every guest I host walks away with all of that and hopefully more!

My life motto is kinda dorky (it's from Dr. Seuss) but I guess sometimes we all just need a little reminder that... You have brains in your head. You have feet in your shoes. You can steer yourself in any direction you choose.

Which of these appealed most to you?

Whilst there is nothing "wrong" with the first, it lacks personality, color and depth. It does little in overcoming potential concerns prospective guests may have in committing to travel great distances and at great expense to stay in a complete stranger's home.

The second profile introduces you, even if only briefly, to someone that looks like a real human being with interests and personality.

These reassuring attributes are intended to paint a picture of the type of experience the guest is likely to have if choosing to stay at that host's place.

To create (or edit) your profile description:
1. Login to Airbnb
2. Click on your account profile photo in the top right corner
3. Select **Edit Profile**
4. Write your profile description in the **Describe Yourself** input box within the **Required** section

Principles

When developing your profile description, try incorporate the following principles...

Tell Your Story: Tell people where you're from, where you've been, and how you got to where you are now. Prospective guests take comfort in knowing that just like them, you too have been on the move in the past.

Share "Insignificant" Details: We all have idiosyncrasies and peculiarities, and exposing yours to a complete stranger will do wonders in helping to break down barriers that creates a sense of intimacy and connection. Your obsession with collecting fridge magnets may make you the butt of jokes amongst your friends, but proves you to be a person of interests and passions no matter how silly they may seem to others.

Focus on Travel: Remember who's reading your profile: Travelers. Sharing your thoughts on what you look for in a life partner might be good for a dating website, but telling Airbnb guests about where you've traveled and what good travel experiences mean to you will do wonders for building rapport. Share travel stories and positive Airbnb experiences that you've had in the past. Let prospective guests know that you've been in their shoes and understand what they're looking for from their Airbnb experience too.

Write for Your Intended Audience: Think about the type of guest most likely to stay in your place. Are they business people? Families? Gap-year backpackers? What kind of host are they most likely to connect with, and what sort of experience are they likely looking for? The way you communicate your values and ideals will be interpreted differently by different people. Your profile description represents an opportunity to connect with your target guests as well as weed out prospective guests that you may wish to avoid attracting too.

Demonstrate Reliability and Maturity: It's a fair assumption that if you're a well-liked person in your day-to-day life, that these attributes are likely to be consistent across all other areas of your life too, with hosting on Airbnb being one other such place. Mention your day job, volunteer associations you're a part of or positions of leadership that demonstrate your maturity and credibility.

Profile Photo

All hosts are required to have a profile photo. Make yours count!

Airbnb enable you to upload multiple photos, although only the first will be your designated profile photo.

There are many perspectives on what the critical ingredients are of a good profile photo: Some say don't look too formal, whilst others say don't be too casual. Some say surround yourself with friends and family, whilst others insist you should be the only one in the shot. Some say to show yourself amidst a fun environment, whilst others say not to let your surroundings dominate the focus of *you* in the picture.

Airbnb encourage uploading frontal face portrait photos that clearly show your face. But aside from this basic guidance, what's the right approach?

The reality is that the *right* approach is simply to avoid the *wrong* approach. And the wrong approach is anything that detracts from building trust and confidence with prospective guests.

Your profile photo needs to instil a level of trust and confidence in guests that are yet to meet you and see first-hand how great you actually are. How you go about achieving this can be done in a multitude of different ways.

To make the point, let's play a small game…

From these photos, ask yourself… which of these hosts' homes would you feel comfortable staying in, and which would you not? (HINT: They're all the same person!)

Did some of the photos invoke trust, likability and rapport whilst others invited doubt, worry or concern?

Repeat this exercise, and for the same photos, pretend that you are now a *gap-year backpacker*, *businessperson* and *senior traveler*. Did this change your level of comfort with the potential host? Probably so.

What this should highlight is the overarching need to be conscious of the type of guest you're trying to attract and ensuring that your profile photo creates the necessary level of trust required for them to hit the *Book Now* button on Airbnb. How you go about doing this is entirely up to you.

To edit your profile photo:

1. Login to Airbnb
2. Click on your account profile photo in the top right corner
3. Select **Profile**
4. Select **Edit Profile** (next to profile picture)
5. Select **Photos and Video** from the menu on the left
6. Click the **Upload a file from your computer** button

Profile Video

Airbnb profile videos are an under-utilized feature that enable Airbnb hosts to let their personalities shine through. They allow hosts to demonstrate to prospective guests that they are in fact *real* and *likable* people.

The benefit of video is the raw honesty that is part and parcel of the medium itself. Words can be edited. Pictures can be cropped. And whilst video can be altered, it inevitably invites prospective guests to come as close as possible to experiencing a personal interaction with their potential host before actually committing to staying at their place.

For prospective guests sitting on the fence with their decision of where they want to stay, adding a video to your profile will give you a head start on competing hosts also being considered.

You only have 30 seconds, so it really is a case of *less is more*. Before hitting the record button, take a moment to make sure you've thought through what you want to communicate to ensure you use each of those valuable seconds for their full potential.

Airbnb recommend focusing on the following topics:
- Where are you from?
- What are some of your interests?
- What do you do in your spare time?
- What is a fun fact about yourself?
- What are some of your favorite things?

Don't worry if you're not happy with your video – you'll get a chance to preview it before it uploads or re-record it until you're satisfied.

And don't worry if your video feels a little *raw* too – this is actually a good thing, and will do wonders in helping guests feel comfortable with you becoming the host of their upcoming trip.

To create a profile video:
1. Login to Airbnb
2. Click on your account profile photo in the top right corner
3. Select **Profile**
4. Select **Edit Profile** (next to profile picture)
5. Select **Photos and Video** from the menu on the left
6. Click the **Record a new video** button

Use Headings and Bullets

It's a little trick that makes a big difference: Use headings and bullets throughout your Airbnb listing.

Benefits of Using Headings and Bullet Points:

- Standing out from the crowd
- Breaking information down into its component parts
- Looking professional and credible
- Highlighting all key points and facts
- Encouraging your audience to read until the end

See what we did there?

Headings and bullet points help the brain digest information quickly, simply and without getting overwhelmed.

You need to remember that prospective guests are most likely looking at many other listings at the same time they're looking at yours. These guests simply won't take the time to sit there and read through long, dense and heavy blocks of text.

The easier you make their job in understanding why your place is the best option, the greater the likelihood that prospective guests will request to book it.

Compare the *Poor Example* vs. *Best Practice* examples on pages 118-119 to see this principle in practice.

Photos

They say that a picture tells a thousand words, and Airbnb is no different. Including photos of all the spaces a guest can use helps them imagine what it'll actually be like to stay at your place.

Your photos are the first thing prospective guests look at and are frequently the decisive factor in determining with whom they wish to book.

Listings with bad photos will struggle to even stand a chance. And the best copy in your listing descriptions will count for nothing if your photos aren't appealing enough to make guests want to learn more.

Compare the following example listings:

Listing A

VS.

Listing B

Which listing would you prefer to stay at? Guess what... they're the same place!

Having professional-grade Airbnb photos from day one is therefore highly recommended. This becomes especially important with the knowledge that many of your competitors have all but likely already done so themselves.

Airbnb offer hosts the option of a paid professional photography shoot for their homes, providing them with at least 12 photos of their space.

The shoot varies in price depending on the size and location of the home. Hosts receive a quote online prior to committing to the service. Once Airbnb match the host with a photographer, the shoot is scheduled directly with the photographer.

After the shoot, the review process can then take up to a month. Hosts can still list their space with their own photos while they wait for their professional photos. Once the photos are approved, Airbnb will deduct the total cost of the photoshoot from the next scheduled payouts until the full amount is collected.

To get a quote and schedule a professional Airbnb photo shoot for your place, visit **www.airbnb.com/info/photography**.

Preparing Your Home to be Photographed

Whether you're booked in for a professional Airbnb photography shoot or taking the snaps yourself, there are a number of things you're able to do to optimize the way your home presents and ensure your photos come out looking great.

If a professional Airbnb photographer turns up to your place, they'll spend somewhere between 30-60 minutes doing their thing. It's still your responsibility for ensuring that you set your photographer up for success by preparing your home to have it shot looking its best.

Below are tips for preparing each key area of your home to be photographed...

The Exterior of Your Home

- Landscape (mow the lawn, trim the shrubs, rake the leaves, pull weeds, etc.)
- Remove garden hoses, sprinklers and garden tools
- Move garbage and recycling cans out of sight
- Move cars from the driveway
- Close the garage door

Bedrooms

- Do not stuff things under the bed if it's in any way visible
- Remove bedside table items (e.g. books, tissues, etc.)
- Ensure any open closets are neat and tidy
- Make beds like they do in hotels
- Add decorative pillows

The Kitchen

- Remove dishes, cleaning products and dish towels from the sink
- Clean major appliances and wipe down counter-tops
- Remove everything from the fridge (e.g. magnets)
- Remove everything (appliances excepted) from kitchen counter-tops
- Remove visible child-proof equipment

The Dining Room

- Set the table using good dinnerware and decorative place settings
- Add a centrepiece (e.g. flowers or candles)
- Dust and polish tabletop
- Conceal electrical cables
- Space chairs evenly

The Living Room

- Arrange furniture in a way that shows off any communal and connected space
- Remove newspapers and magazines
- Hide remote controls from sight
- Conceal electrical cables
- Fluff furniture pillows

The Local Neighborhood

Whilst not part of your home, make sure to include a few photos (two to three) of key landmarks or attractions from your local area. These can be of any points of interest that showcase your neighborhood in its best light.

Taking Photos Yourself

Airbnb's professional photography service may not be available in your local area. Even if it is, you may still wish to take photos yourself, or do so while you wait to receive your professional Airbnb photos (which can take a few months).

If you decide to take photos yourself, here are a few tips used by the pros when taking professional photos:

De-clutter your space: That collection of magazines from the last three years might be sentimental to you, but probably not so to guests. Create an environment that maintains your personality whilst still remaining "neutral" enough for guests to imagine themselves living in.

Get clever with angles: Photographers typically take photos of rooms from the doorway, capturing any windows and room features from this angle. Keep this in mind when arranging furniture and styling the room in preparation for your shoot.

Brighten up the inside: Shoot during the day and open all blinds and curtains. Make sure to turn on all lights (including surface lights like those on your stove) before taking any photos and replace any burned out light bulbs. Focus the camera away from windows wherever possible and ensure that flashes do not show up as reflections on reflective surfaces.

Fake it till you make it: Your guests can't turn up to a place that looks different to the photos they've seen online. But putting your best foot forward is absolutely fine. Little staging tricks like displaying fruit bowls, flowers and coffee table books go a long way in taking things up a notch.

One photo per room: As a rule of thumb, take one photo of each room that guests will have access to. Remember that prospective guests aren't yet familiar with your place, so make sure they understand the space and everything it has to offer.

Highlight unique features: Take photos of anything that sets your place apart from other homes and hotels. Highlight unique amenities and capture anything that fills your home with life and personality.

Composition: Use the rule of thirds – the idea that an image should be imagined as divided into nine equal parts, made by two equally spaced horizontal lines and two equally spaced vertical lines. Important compositional elements should be placed along these lines or their intersections.

Shoot into a corner: Do not shoot flat onto a wall. This will make a space seem smaller than it is in real life. Shooting into a corner will show a broad range of space, add some depth and help give a sense of true perspective.

Vertical Lines: Ensure that all vertical lines such as door frames and cupboards remain vertical and do not appear to lean on an angle. Using a tripod to ensure your camera is 100% level when shooting will achieve this.

Time of Day: The best time to shoot outdoors is the first and last hour of the day's sunlight.

Resolution: Take high-resolution photos that are at least 1024 x 683 pixels. Bigger is always better.

Orientation: Wherever possible, take photos in landscape (in favor of portrait) orientation. Whilst there's nothing wrong with portrait-oriented photos, a photo should ideally be composed based on its intended display medium. In the case of Airbnb, photos simply look better when displayed in landscape orientation.

Equipment You'll Want: Have a friend that's an amateur professional photographer? Recruit their help in exchange for a home cooked meal or nice bottle of wine. Try get your hands on some photography equipment essentials: A good DSLR camera, tripod, electronic flash and wide-angle lenses (faster lenses are preferable for photographing indoors).

To add additional photos to your listing:
1. Login to Airbnb
2. In **Hosting** mode, select **Listings** from the top navigation bar
3. Select **Manage listing** for your listing
4. Click on **Listing details** from the menu at the top
5. Click the **Edit** button for the **Photos** section
6. Scroll to the bottom and click within the **Add another** rectangle

Photo Captions

Photo captions help prospective guests imagine what sort of experience they will have in your place. They can be just as important as the copy in your listing descriptions, and help prospective guests imagine themselves actually staying at your place.

Using the previous example photos, compare the following photo captions...

Master bedroom

vs.

Experience spaciousness and breathing room... a rare commodity for New York City apartments

Bedroom with walk-in closet

vs.

Recluse to your own personal space whilst the family entertain themselves in the room right next door!

Living room

vs.

Gaze out at the Empire State Building whilst unwinding in your very own oversized lounge

Before they know it, guests are picturing themselves staring out at the Empire State Building whilst unwinding on an oversized lounge as they hit the *Book Now* button.

Sequence and Number of Photos

The order and number of photos matters. You'll want to use your photos to create the closest thing possible to a guided tour of your place. Do so by sequencing your photos in an order that makes its way logically through your house.

Hosts frequently start with the most captivating photo which is commonly the master bedroom or lounge room.

Photos
Add photos that show guests what your place looks like.

Remember that the first photo will also be your "showcase" photo that gets displayed in search results and at the top of your listing page (see page 82 for an example of this). Make sure it counts!

Do not duplicate photos of the same room unless the extra photos show-off additional features or selling points not seen in other photos.

Typically, 15 photos (give or take) is considered a good number to include.

Elements of an Airbnb Listing

In the past, travelers were limited in their options for accommodation: Stay in a hotel, hostel or traditional bed & breakfast. And whilst the concept of providing four-walls-and-a-roof to travelers is far from unique to Airbnb, each and every place listed on Airbnb is peppered with the flavors of the host, their home and the local neighborhood.

So what does this actually look like? It may be comic book fans that aren't shy to display their collection of Superman figurines in every corner of their home. Maybe it's a beachside bungalow that embraces its surroundings through color, decor and furnishings. Or urban retreats that organically adapt to their hustle-and-bustle metropolis surroundings.

Guests frequently select their Airbnb in the hope of being exposed to unique experiences and local flavors. Many are looking beyond just *price* in their selection process.

Your listing needs to be crystal clear in communicating...

- What kind of place you have
- What kind of experience you will provide to guests
- Why you love where you live; and
- Why guests will appreciate choosing your place over other alternatives

As the sole mechanism for providing prospective guests with an insight into what it might be like to stay at your place (and all the reasons your place is better than others they may also be considering), your Airbnb listing represents the vital link between simply being *listed* and actually getting *booked.*

Prospective guests are yet to see your home and have not personally met you – they have only what they read on your listing to go by in deciding where they want to stay.

There are different elements of an Airbnb listing – everything from the listing name, through to a summary of the space and the local neighborhood.

Getting each of these elements right is critical to slowly edging prospective guests closer and closer towards the necessary comfort they need to feel before booking your place. The risk of losing them at any point on this journey cannot be emphasized enough.

There's a lot to get right in building an effective Airbnb listing that generates reservation requests. This represents both an opportunity and a challenge: Get it right and you set yourself up for long-term success on Airbnb. Get it wrong and you risk becoming another anonymous listing amidst a sea of competition. Make sure you seize the opportunity.

To truly give your Airbnb listing depth and color, you should complete each of the sections available to you.

You have the ability to provide additional details for each of the following sections of your listing:

Listing Name: A high-level summary of what makes your place uniquely great

Listing Summary: A brief overview of the key selling points of your place

The Space: Information about all the different areas and amenities within your place

Guest Access: An overview of the spaces that guests will have access to within your home

Interaction With Guests: Information on how you'll be available to offer help and/or socialize throughout the stay

Other Things to Note: Other details that may impact a guest's stay (for better or worse)

Neighborhood Overview: Information on what makes your local area great or unique and any key local attractions

Getting Around: Information on public transport, driving and walking options

Each of these sections is overviewed in greater detail across the subsequent pages.

Listing Name

The aim of your listing name is to make your listing stand out from other listings in search results, enough to make prospective guests want to click through and take a look at your listing page.

There is a 50 character count limit.

Tips and tricks:

- Don't waste your precious 50 character count limit on things that prospective guests can learn elsewhere (e.g. the number of bedrooms or bathrooms)
- Highlight your differentiating attributes (e.g. is it family-friendly? Close to the city? Free access to gym facilities?)
- Remain conscious of your target guests and the type of travelers most likely to be interested in your place. Make sure to tailor your listing name to their particular interests

Poor Example:

3 bedroom, 2 bathroom apartment

Best Practice Example:

Family-friendly Dream NYC Apartment

Examples

Here are a few listing names for top-performing Airbnb's from all around the world:

Sunny Studio Close to San Telmo
Buenos Aires, Argentina

Perfect Escape Sunny Roof EnSuite
Bangkok, Thailand

Modern Luxury Close to Beach, City and Transport
Sydney, Australia

Luxury design apt w spacious sunny balcony
London, United Kingdom

Lovely Room, EXCELLENT AREA for Access to all NYC
New York, United States

Romantic Hideout in Paris
Paris, France

Listing Summary

The aim of your listing summary is to provide a teaser that whets the appetite of prospective guests enough to make them want to keep reading the rest of your listing page and descriptions.

There is a 500 character count limit.

Tips and tricks:

- Use bullet points
- Focus on the top-5 impressive and differentiating attributes of your place
- Highlight amenities and features most likely to appeal to your target guests

Poor Example:

The apartment is a big 3 bedroom 2 bathroom apartment in Gramercy (2 rooms are larger). It is already furnished and there is also a big kitchen. It is kept very clean & we are close to everything you would want. It also has a rooftop and an elevator

Best Practice Example:

- Massive 820 square foot 3 bedroom, 2 bathroom with lounge
- Fully-furnished, light and quiet
- Large appliance-stocked kitchen
- Minutes' walk to trains, bus, shops, food and nightlife
- Doorman / elevator building with laundry
- Stunning rooftop view

The Space

The aim of *The Space* section is to provide assurances to prospective guests that all amenities and features of importance to them will be provided at your place.

Tips and tricks:

- Use headings and bullet points
- Breakdown the description of your place into its individual rooms and the sections of your home
- Minimize use of overly-poetic language in preference for clear and simple descriptions

Poor Example:

The space

The apartment has 3 bedrooms and 2 bathrooms. 2 of the bedrooms are bigger than the 3rd bedroom. 2 of the bedrooms have a queen-size bed, and 1 of the bedrooms has a king-size bed. 1 of the bedrooms has an en-suite attached to it – very useful! Each of the bathrooms have a toilet, shower and bathtub. The apartment also has air-conditioning and heating.

There's a really big kitchen with pretty much everything you would want in a kitchen, like a microwave, oven and even a dishwasher.

In the building there is also a laundry room in the basement. The building also has a doorman, and an elevator which is neat!

Best Practice Example:

The space

THE BUILDING
- Brand-new 23-story luxury rental building
- 24-hour doorman
- Magnificent 20-foot artfully-crafted marble lobby
- Laundry room with washing machines and dryers
- Hallways elegantly carpeted and wallpapered
- On-level garbage and recycling chute

APARTMENT AMENITIES
- Double-glazed, insulated, sound dampening windows
- Hardwood oak floors

THE BEDROOMS
- Room 1: 180 square foot space with en-suite bathroom, queen-size bed, television, walk-in closet, dresser, bedside table, desk and couch
- Room 2: 180 square foot space with king-size bed, walk-in closet, 2 dressers, bedside table and desk
- Room 3: 120 square foot space with queen-size bed and 2 dressers
- Air-conditioning / heating units in each bedroom

THE LOUNGE ROOM
- Large 100 square foot space
- Surround-sound television and entertainment unit
- 4-person super-comfy sofa
- Air-conditioning / heating unit

THE BATHROOMS
- 2 superbly-appointed bathrooms; each containing: Toilet, shower with detachable head, bathtub, vanity with basin, extended mirrors and cupboard storage space

THE ROOFTOP
- Incredible high-rise view of city
- Uninterrupted views of Freedom Tower, Empire State and Chrysler Buildings

Guest Access

The aim of the *Guest Access* section is to maximize perceptions of personal space, and access to amenities and home features that would be desired by guests.

Tips and tricks:

- Overtly state all of the areas that guests will have access to
- Make mention of things that guests would appreciate having access to (even if they seem obvious)
- Explicitly encourage guests to feel at home and use all amenities they are granted access to within your place

Poor Example:

Guest access

The entire apartment is yours. You can also use the laundry room and go on the roof

Best Practice Example:

Guest access

ACCESS TO EVERYTHING – FEEL LIKE IT'S YOUR HOME:
- Complete and uninterrupted access to all areas of entire apartment
- Access to in-building laundry room (with washing machine and dryer)
- Access to rooftop

Interaction with Guests

The aim of the *Interaction with Guests* section is to eliminate any apprehensions prospective guests may have around a smooth-sailing guest experience, and providing comfort that their preferences for personal space and socialization will be respected.

Tips and tricks:

- Include an introductory statement that recognizes the importance of a problem-free travel experience
- Let prospective guests know all the ways you ensure guest concerns are taken care of
- State all the ways you're happy to be contacted before, throughout and after the guest's stay

Poor Example:

Interaction with guests

I'll meet you at the apartment and give you the keys

Best Practice Example:

Interaction with guests

I like to ensure your vacation starts off on the right foot. I will personally greet you upon arrival at the building. To ensure your every concern is put to rest, I also like to introduce you to the doorman. Once you've had a chance to drop your bags and grab a drink, I'm always happy to give you a quick walk-through of the local area. If you're not up to it, I'm equally happy to run you through a list of key attractions and "cheat sheets" for making the most of your stay.

As a long-time local, I'm well-placed to recommend the best attractions, advise on the best ways of getting around or offer suggestions for anything that might pop up during your stay. I'm only ever a phone call away! Also feel free to drop me an email anytime – I'm at the computer so often anyways.

And if you're anything like me, you'll forget half your luggage in the mad scramble back to the airport. Don't worry – this has happened 2983492934 times before (especially with kids!) and we always find a way to get your prized possessions back into your hot little hands.

Other Things to Note

The aim of the *Other Things to Note* section is to call out any other details that may impact a guest's stay, for better or for worse.

Tips and Tricks:

- Explicitly mention any additional amenities or features likely to be of interest
- Highlight the importance of having a positive travel experience
- Invite the opportunity to open up communication channels for further discussion

Poor Example:

Other things to note

The garbage chute can be accessed in the trash room which is at the end of the corridor and to the right

Best Practice Example:

Other things to note

Your enjoyment in my home is my PRIMARY concern.

Here are a few things we think you'll want to know...

WELCOME BASKET: You'll arrive to a welcome basket inclusive of milk, cereals, chips, cheese and crackers, sodas and juice-boxes, chocolates, popcorn and other yummy snacks

COFFEE AND TEA: Premium coffee machine with wide selection of flavors, as well as assortment of teas provided free-of-charge

COOKING BASICS: Help yourself to condiments (such as jam, peanut butter, ketchup, mustard, etc.) as well as sugar, salt, olive oil, vinegar and a selection of herbs and spices – all provided complementary for your stay

GARBAGE AND RECYCLING: There is a garbage chute and recycle room located right next to the apartment

PARKING: There is unmetered all-day street parking in the streets around the apartment. There is also a secure parking garage on-site. Regrettably, the garage fits small to medium-sized cars only

MAINTENANCE: The building has on-site maintenance. Speak to the doorman 24/7 to report any issues for immediate repair

Don't be shy to contact me if you have any questions about the home or local area. I love to help my guests!

Neighborhood Overview

The aim of the *Neighborhood Overview* section is to let guests know why your neighborhood is better than other alternatives they may also be considering.

Tips and Tricks:

- Use bullet points
- Overview your neighborhood's key selling points and proximity to places of interest, key landmarks, attractions and public transport
- Using both *content* and *language*, overview the type of places that your target guests would be most interested in

Poor Example:

The neighborhood

The apartment is in the Gramercy neighborhood. Getting around is pretty easy since the 6 train is very close to the apartment, and Union Square station is not too much further either. There are a ton of great tourist sites that are close by to the apartment, and a lot of great places to go out and eat around the apartment too.

Best Practice Example:

The neighborhood

- Located in the beautiful Gramercy neighborhood and a couple of blocks away from trains (4, 5, 6, L, N, Q and R lines) and buses that'll take you anywhere uptown, downtown, crosstown and into Brooklyn
- No more than 15 minute walk to the Empire State Building, Union Square, Herald Square, Flatiron Building, Madison Square Park and East River
- Never more than 30 minutes away from neighborhoods like Greenwich Village, West Village, Chelsea, SoHo, Chinatown, Lower East Side, Times Square, Grand Central Station or any other downtown or midtown spot
- Located in the heart of countless bars, restaurants, shops and central transport hubs
- Easy to get to by cab or public transport from JFK, LaGuardia and Newark airports

Getting Around

The aim of the *Getting Around* section is to provide assurances to guests that getting around will be simple and uncomplicated.

Tips and Tricks:

- Explain all of the various public transport options (trains, buses, cabs, ferry and driving) that guests have easy access to from your place
- Let guests know where the public transport options will take them (as opposed to just stating what the options are)
- State the proximity and travel time involved in getting to each of the public transport options

Poor Example:

Getting around

Getting around is really easy from the apartment. The 6 train is really close

Best Practice Example:

Getting around

TRAINS: 5min walk to 6 line (taking you anywhere on the East side of Manhattan) and 10min walk to L, 4, 5, N, Q and R lines (taking you uptown, downtown, crosstown and into Brooklyn)

BUSES: 5min walk to multiple buses that go up and down 1st, 2nd and 3rd Avenue as well as crosstown (at 23rd Street)

CABS / UBERS: Readily available cabs and Ubers constantly driving past building and surrounding streets

FERRY: 15min walk to East River Ferry at 35th Street

PARKING: Parking lot located one block away

House Rules

You have the option of setting house rules for your guests. Your house rules let prospective guests know how you expect them to behave when staying at your place.

There's no penalty for cancelling if guests break your rules. However hosts who set fewer rules tend to get more reservations.

Airbnb provide a few common suggested rules you may wish to set. You are also able to add any other rules you choose yourself:

House Rules

All guests will agree to your House Rules before sending a reservation request.

Suitable for children (2-12 years) *	✕ ✓
Suitable for infants (under 2 years) *	✕ ✓
Pets allowed	✕ ✓
Smoking allowed	✕ ✓
Parties and events allowed	✕ ✓

* Guests of all ages are welcome on Airbnb. Only choose "No" if your home has features that may pose a risk of harm to children or damage to property. In this case, guests will still be able to reachout for more details. Learn more

Additional rules

You can include any requirements around safety concerns, shared space rules, and your community regulations, as well as rules like: "No solo travlers" or "Quiet time after 10pm".

Save   Cancel

Additional rules can cover anything that's important that you'd like your guests to know. This includes things like areas of your home that are out-of-bounds or permission to have visitors.

Your house rules appear on your listing page so that guests can review them before requesting to book. This has the benefit of allowing hosts to be upfront in their expectations, as well as eliminating any surprises that guests only learn about to their disappointment throughout their stay.

Despite these benefits, it also has the potential to scare off guests that are considering staying at your place too. Being too heavy-handed with your house rules gives prospective guests the impression that you're the kind of host that's likely to be overbearing (even if the rules themselves are fair).

Therefore, the purpose of your house rules should simply be to increase transparency and clarity around your expectations. You'll want to use your house rules as an opportunity to demonstrate your commitment to providing consistently positive experiences for *all* of your guests. Prospective guests should ideally see your house rules as an effort to create a great space that *they* **will benefit from as much as** *you* **will**.

Principles

Limit the Number of Rules You Mention

Section XXVII of the *Clean Streets Act* may state that "Dropping litter on the footpath will incur a $50 on-the-spot fine". There's little wiggle-room for one to argue they weren't clear on what the rule was, or what the punishment will be for breaking it.

Your house rules are a little different.

House rules primarily establish the expectations you have of guests to eliminate any surprises that may arise throughout the duration of their stay.

Whilst you're theoretically able to cancel a booking without penalty if a guest breaks your rule, it'll be a drawn-out and unpleasant process to bring into effect, and a scenario you'll want to avoid if at all possible.

You may also find it a little hard to define a definitive list of things that *are* and *are not* permitted within your place.

With all of this in mind, any attempt to build an exhaustive list of *every* possible rule that covers *every* possible contingency is an exercise doomed to fail. This problem is compounded by the risk of putting off guests by coming across as too heavy-handed with too many rules.

You therefore need to be selective in the house rules you choose to include. Limit these to the top three to five most important rules to you, if you decide to include any at all.

Don't Dump Everything in House Rules

What constitutes a *rule* is a broad concept.

For example, is your maximum occupancy a potential house rule? Yes, but it is also something you're able to specify as a *booking setting*.

It is important to be selective in what you choose to classify as a "house rule". There may be things you consciously omit so you don't give the impression of being an overbearing host.

Reserve precious house rule "real estate" exclusively for things that can't be dealt with elsewhere.

Consider also whether you're able to communicate any of these things during pre-arrival communications, the check-in process, in House Manuals you develop, or other sections of your listing page (such as the *Other Things to Note* section).

Ensure that you save your house rules exclusively for calling out any critical expectations that prospective guests need to be aware of prior to booking your place and which can't be called out anywhere else.

Limiting Rules are Better than Blanket Rules

As we've established, nobody *likes* rules. However rules need not be only black or white - there can be *grades* of rules too. And a partial rule is better than a blanket rule.

For example, you may have had bad experiences in granting guests access to the kitchen. Maybe they failed to clean up after themselves? Maybe this caused you to get bugs? And maybe all of this caused frustrations with other roommates or guests?

The knee-jerk reaction would be to simply implement a rule that forebode guests having access to the kitchen. Problem solved? Yes. But a little heavy-handed? Probably so.

Given the problem you're trying to avoid, what if the rule were simply a requirement that guests clean up after themselves if using the kitchen? This would seem reasonable and unobjectionable to your common guest as well as solve the problem you're trying to avoid.

Be Conscious of Guest Types

You wouldn't explain road rules to your five year old child in the same way you'd be discussing them with your teenager that's learning to drive.

Your audience matters in how you phrase your rules. This comes down to the type of guest you most commonly attract to your place.

For example, to an ethical traveler, your request to switch off the lights and air-conditioner when not in use could be phrased as being to help the environment. This is something they'd most likely willingly support.

Make sure that whenever describing your rules, you put yourself in the shoes of your target guests. Eliminate as many objections as you're able to pre-empt by phrasing the rule in a way that will resonate and sit best with them.

Target guests are covered in greater detail on page 96 of the *Building the Perfect Listing* chapter.

W.I.I.F.M. (What's In It For Me?)

With a sea of choices on Airbnb, guests have a wide selection when deciding which place will be best for them. As paying customers, they'll inevitably frame this decision around the question: *What's in it for me?*

They'll do this on multiple occasions throughout the process of deciding where they want to stay. And the influence of house rules on these decisions cannot be emphasized enough.

Your job is to explain what benefits your guests stand to *gain* – not *lose* – through your rules. When done correctly, this will transform your rules into something that has the potential to enhance, not hinder, their travel experience.

As an example, you may have a rule requiring guests to switch off all lights, air-conditioning and heating when they leave your house. Your primary motivation will most likely be to minimize your electricity costs. Through phrasing this cleverly, you can position this rule as principally being for the guest's benefit: Lower electricity costs = lower Airbnb overheads = savings you're able to pass on to them.

When explained in this way, guests will more likely be understanding of your house rules once they appreciate what's in it for them.

Reciprocity

An offshoot of the W.I.I.F.M. principle, is reciprocity – the idea that people are willing to give back the kind of treatment they receive.

This becomes especially important when what you're offering on Airbnb is a *shared* or *private* room (i.e. living with others).

When done correctly, you'll transform your house rule from an edict you're imposing onto guests into a level playing field where guest and host are equals.

Examples

Hosts often ask for examples of the type of house rules they should think about including on their Airbnb listings. Below is a summary of some common rule categories you may wish to include.

Do not view this as an exhaustive list that *must* be added in its entirety to the house rules section of your Airbnb listing. Rather, select the two or three that may be of most importance and relevance to you.

A problem-free track-record may indicate a lack of needing to implement any house rules at all. If this is the case for you, then view these examples as rules to keep up your sleeve for a time you feel it necessary to implement at your place:

- **Access:** Are there prohibitions on any areas that guests are and aren't allowed access to?
- **Amenities:** Are there any rules for using any amenities or features of your home?
- **Behavior:** Do you have any expectations around the ways guests should be behaving within your space?
- **Cleanliness:** Are there any cleaning or cleanliness expectations?
- **Damage:** What are your expectations around spills or damage to property and being informed about incidents and accidents that take place?
- **Drugs:** What actions will be taken if illicit drugs are consumed on the property?
- **Electricity:** What expectations or requirements do you have around lights, air-conditioning and heating being used?
- **Noise:** What limitations are there around making noise, the volume that music can be played, or the times that guests are expected to be quieter?
- **Security:** Are there requirements to keep doors, gates or certain areas locked?

Ensure that any rules you decide to include comply with Airbnb's Non-Discrimination policy.

Pricing Your Place

The Importance of Developing a Robust Pricing Strategy

The principle rationale for why people choose to list their homes on Airbnb cannot be forgotten when deciding how much to charge for your place. For most Airbnb hosts, this is to **make money**.

Having an effective pricing strategy that takes full advantage of the financial opportunities afforded by Airbnb is therefore critical to seeing Airbnb as a worthwhile investment of your time and energy.

With so many different ways you're able to price your place, many hosts often feel overwhelmed and unsure of where to even start. They often feel that they're missing opportunities to maximize their full earning potential.

Sadly, many of them are right.

When it comes to pricing on Airbnb, your goal is to find your pricing *sweet spot* – the amount you're able to charge that ensures you're not missing any opportunities by *over-charging* or *under-quoting* at any point in time.

Pricing correctly on Airbnb can be a confusing and overwhelming activity. Yet for the very same reasons, getting your pricing right will position you head-and-shoulders above your competition.

Having an awareness of your competitors' prices and being familiar with your various pricing options represents the recipe for success for maximizing your Airbnb earning potential.

Smart Pricing and Price Tips

When you first setup your Airbnb listing, Airbnb offered you the option of setting your price to dynamically adapt to demand (see page 90).

Airbnb introduced the Smart Pricing tool to help hosts overcome their pricing "blind spots". Smart Pricing lets you set your prices to automatically go up or down to match demand in your market, but only within the price range you choose.

The Airbnb Smart Pricing tool uses a trove of data like local demand, your amenities, previous bookings, the number of people who view your listing, and how often you'd like to host, to recommend optimal nightly prices you're able to charge for your place.

The easiest way to think about how the Smart Pricing tool (and Price Tips) works is to think about how hotels charge different prices for different nights...

- A hotel in Tokyo knows it can charge a lot more for a room while the Olympic Games are being hosted in Japan than during other times
- A hotel knows it has a longer timeframe to gradually reduce the price of un-booked nights six months out from today than it does one week out from today
- A hotel knows how booked out they and other hotels in the local area are, and the availability of alternative accommodation options that exist for guests looking for somewhere to stay

Smart Pricing and Price Tips work in the same way.

Airbnb have far greater visibility than individual hosts over all the factors that indicate current levels of supply and demand, as well as the relationship of these variables to listings such as yours.

Airbnb do not release the specific algorithm they use to calculate their price tip recommendations. They have however released general information on some of the factors they will consider:

- **Searches:** If searches for listings like yours go up (e.g. for a peak day of the week, season, event or holiday), price tips will rise to match the demand.

- **Availability:** Price tips factor in open nights on your listing's calendar. If fewer nights are available, price tips tend to be higher.

- **Time left to book:** If the price tip dates are weeks or months away, prices can be higher. But if the time left to book is running out and the listing hasn't been booked, price tips will lower to help attract bookings.

- **Your listing's qualities:** Price tips factor in your listing's location, room type, number of guests, amenities, and reviews.

It takes all of these factors (and others) into consideration to then determine a nightly price that strikes the optimal balance between maximizing your number of bookings with charging an appropriate amount for each of those bookings.

In some instances, the pricing tool may recommend **charging less** than you may think you're able to charge. It will do so based on how often you've told Airbnb you want to host ("as often as possible" vs. "part-time") and then reducing your rates in a way that best achieves those goals.

In other instances, it may recommend **charging more** for your *Hawaiian beach-side villa* during summer where demand is naturally going to be higher.

Travel trends can change daily

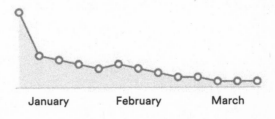

January   February   March

Either way, the Smart Pricing tool is not without its critics. Is it your best option for maximizing your Airbnb earning potential? Here's the case both *for* and *against...*

The Case For

Let's assume that Airbnb, like all other businesses, is motivated by maximizing their profitability. Airbnb's business model is premised on being brokers that facilitate short-term rentals and take a small cut from every reservation they facilitate.

The logic would be that the more reservations they facilitate, the more reservations they take a commission from. And similarly, the more you charge for each of those reservations, the greater the service fee they're able to take from each of those reservations too.

Therefore, whether through maximizing bookings or your nightly rate – every time you make money as a host, so too will Airbnb.

Airbnb further claim that when a host selects a price that's within 5% of their price tip recommendations, those hosts are nearly 4x more likely to get booked, in comparison to hosts whose prices are more than 5% off from Airbnb's recommendations. They also claim that hosts that have followed their pricing recommendations have lifted their earnings by an average of 13%.

The Case Against

Guest Discounts vs. Host Profitability

Some critics point out that this simple overview fails to recognize a small, but important distinction: The difference in service fees that Airbnb take from hosts versus guests.

Airbnb aim to keep two distinct user groups happy:

1. **Hosts:** Airbnb want to ensure that hosts see Airbnb as a lucrative source of income
2. **Guests:** Airbnb want to ensure that guests see Airbnb as their go-to option for short-term rental accommodation

These two objectives are in direct competition with one another.

Airbnb charge a flat service fee of **3% from hosts** for all reservations, irrespective of size or duration. In contrast, **service fees for guests range between 6-12%**.

From a purely financial perspective (3% host service fees vs. 6-12% guest service fees), there is more for Airbnb to gain by recommending lower prices that keep guests happy (and booking more frequently on Airbnb).

Keeping guests "happy" (with lower prices) inevitably comes at the expense of hosts' abilities to charge more for their places, since it requires *more reservations* at *lower prices* (rather than less reservations at higher prices).

This dynamic is supported by anecdotal evidence from seasoned Airbnb hosts who've observed that the prices they're able to command from their listings are above the prices that Airbnb recommend they charge when using the Smart Pricing tool.

Tips Lack Specificity to Your Listing

As a second limitation, Airbnb provide only "generalized" pricing recommendations for listings that are *like* yours as opposed to *your* specific listing.

Your two bedroom, one bathroom apartment in New York may be much nicer than other two bedroom, one bathroom apartments of inferior quality also in New York. If that's the case, you deserve to command higher prices for your place because of this fact. The opposite is also true should your place be of *inferior* quality to other two bedroom, one bathroom apartments.

Whilst Airbnb's Smart Pricing tool will take some of your home's unique attributes into account, it is not nuanced enough to fully-address this limitation. It will consequently pigeonhole your listing amongst other listings using only a limited set of categorizing attributes.

Lacking in Seasonal Variability

As an offshoot of this, a few minutes of experimentation with Smart Pricing will reveal that Airbnb's price tips lack variability from date-to-date.

As an example, the price it recommends for a Tuesday in winter may be the exact same amount it recommends for a Saturday in summer.

Failing to provide pricing recommendations that change meaningfully at different times of the year can represent significant missed opportunities – especially for places that have wide variance in seasonal supply and demand.

Without true differentiation in prices across different dates and seasons, there's good reason to remain sceptical about the extent to which the tool is truly optimizing your earning potential based on other dynamic factors that stand to benefit you too.

Activating Smart Pricing

If you wish to activate Smart Pricing and didn't already do so when creating your Airbnb listing, you're still able to do so at any time after your listing has gone live:

1. Login to Airbnb
2. In **Hosting** mode, select **Listings** from the top navigation bar
3. Select **Manage listing** for your listing
4. Click on **Pricing** from the menu at the top
5. Click the **Edit** button for the **Nightly price** section
6. Turn **Smart Pricing** to "**On**"
7. Enter your **Minimum price** and **Maximum price** into the input boxes
8. Specify how often you wish to host by choosing either **As often as possible** or **Part-time** under the **How often do you want to host?** section
9. Click the **Save** button

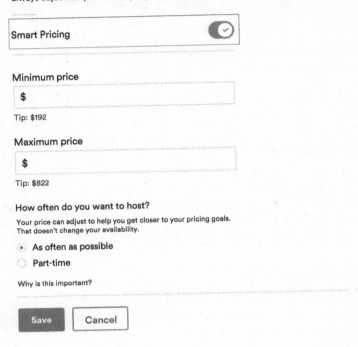

Nightly price

Set your prices to automatically match demand, or choose a fixed price. You can always adjust the price for any night by selecting the date. What is Smart Pricing?

Smart Pricing

Minimum price

$

Tip: $192

Maximum price

$

Tip: $822

How often do you want to host?

Your price can adjust to help you get closer to your pricing goals. That doesn't change your availability.

⦿ As often as possible

◯ Part-time

Why is this important?

Save   Cancel

You're similarly able to deactivate Smart Pricing any time after creating your listing too, by turning **Smart Pricing** to "**Off**" (replacing *Step 6* for *activating* Smart Pricing on the previous page).

Price Tips

Airbnb also offer **Price Tips** for individual days, regardless of whether you've enabled Smart Pricing or not. These are determined using the same methods used by the Smart Pricing tool.

To view your price tips:

1. Login to Airbnb
2. In **Hosting** mode, select **Listings** from the top navigation bar
3. Select **Calendar** for your listing
4. Click on any individual upcoming date and note Airbnb's price tip underneath the **Price for the night** input box

In the example below, Airbnb recommend charging *$346* for the *1st September 2017*:

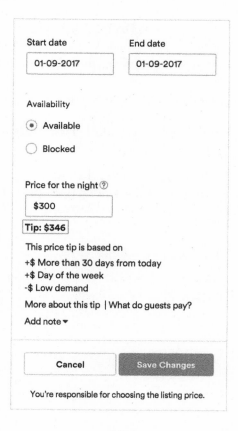

Clicking on the tip (beneath the *Price for the night* input box) will automatically copy and paste the price tip amount into the input box for you. If you want to update the price for the night to Airbnb's price tip, don't forget to *Save Changes*.

Aside from offering nightly price tips for individual days on your calendar, Airbnb will also offer price tips for your:

- Default nightly price
- Minimum and maximum nightly prices
- Long term discounts

Airbnb use a color code for their price tips. This is helpful when looking at your calendar to get a high-level "feel" for how accurately you're pricing compared to what Airbnb suggest you should be pricing at:

COLOR	WHAT IT MEANS
Green	At your current price, you're **likely** to get booked
Yellow	At your current price, you're **less likely** to get booked
Orange	At your current price, you're **least likely** to get booked

When you select a date range (i.e. more than just a single night) on your calendar, Airbnb also provide a **View price tips** option that enables you to see what prices it would recommend instead:

> **Get price tips for these dates**
>
> They're based on demand and personalised for your listing.
>
> View price tips | What do guests pay?

September 2016 ▾

Sun	Mon	Tue	Wed	Thu	Fri	Sat
28	29	30	31	Sep 1	2	3
4	5	6	7	8	9	10
11 $345 ~~$475~~	12 $372 ~~$475~~	13 $365 ~~$475~~	14 $409 ~~$475~~	15 $407 ~~$475~~	16 $433 ~~$475~~	17 $433 ~~$475~~
18 $400 ~~$475~~	19 $407 ~~$475~~	20 $402 ~~$475~~	21 $365 ~~$475~~	22	23	24
25	26 $372 ~~$550~~	27 $372 ~~$550~~	28 $372 ~~$550~~	29 $374 ~~$550~~	30	Oct 1

Once the price tips have been displayed, Airbnb also provide a **Save these prices** button to save Airbnb's proposed recommendations should you wish.

Dynamic Pricing Tools: A More Reliable Alternative

As an Airbnb host, *your* priority is to maximize *your* earning potential (as opposed to providing cheap rental accommodation options for guests). Any price tip recommendations needs to be as specific to *your* individual property, *your* local area and *your* local competition.

Recognizing this and the inherent limitations of Airbnb's Smart Pricing tool, dynamic pricing companies have emerged to provide this specific service. These companies dynamically...

- Monitor prices and occupancy rates of your local competition
- Research key events in your area that impact supply and demand
- Consider seasonality factors; as well as
- Day of the week factors; and
- Time till booking

They combine all of this data to determine optimal dynamic price recommendations that are continually updated as new data continues to come in. They then provide you with price recommendations that optimize your earning potential in a way that you'd never be able to do yourself.

Many of these services integrate directly with your Airbnb account, meaning you don't even need to manually update your pricing – they do it for you automatically.

In short, dynamic pricing services eliminate the need to figure out how much to charge to achieve optimal prices and occupancy for your place at different times of the week, month and year.

These companies charge either a percentage of your Airbnb earnings (typically ranging between 0.5% to 2% of your booking revenue) or a monthly fee (typically between $15-$30 per month).

To see an example of how dynamic pricing works for your listing, check out two of the more popular and reliable dynamic pricing companies: **Beyond Pricing** and **Everbooked.** Both allow you to preview their dynamic pricing tool using your own Airbnb listing.

A Step-By-Step Guide to Pricing Your Place

If you decide not to use Airbnb's Smart Pricing tool or any of the dynamic pricing alternatives, then you'll need to independently determine how much to charge for your place yourself.

Even if you decide to use any of these pricing alternatives, going through the process of determining how much to charge for your place is still a worthwhile exercise to undertake. You will familiarize yourself with your local competition as well as sanity-check that any price tips provided to you are more or less aligned with what you know the opportunity to be.

Pricing your place on Airbnb is a 5-stage process:

1. Researching your local competition
2. Moving away from one-size-fits-all pricing
3. Increasing prices for times of high demand
4. Offering long term discounts
5. Adding extra fees

Each of these steps is broken down in greater detail below...

Step 1: Researching Your Local Competition

Truly successful Airbnb hosts possess a thorough understanding of their local competition and the prices they're able to command on Airbnb.

These hosts are aware of supply and demand in their local area at different times of the year and take advantage of this knowledge to maximize their earning potential.

The default nightly price tip provided to you by Airbnb upon listing your place was calculated using a limited number of factors. Factors considered include things like your location, the number of bedrooms and bathrooms, the type of property you have, what amenities you're offering guests within your space and the number of guests it accommodates.

Whilst criteria like these may seem like they cover a broad range of variables able to group you with other comparable listings, this is unfortunately only partially true.

Think about what all the 3 bedroom, 2 bathroom apartments look like in your city: You'll have luxury apartments, run-down apartments, flashy new apartments in run-down areas, and shabby old apartments in glamorous neighborhoods.

There are natural limits on Airbnb's ability to find listings that are *truly comparable* to yours, without knowing more about your place. No two listings are exactly the same despite commonalities that may exist between them.

Your goal in researching the local competition is to better understand comparable listings in your local area to determine the optimal amount you're able to charge for *your* place.

Very shortly you'll be able to answer the question: *What is my place worth at different times of the year?*

Getting this even *slightly* wrong can represent the "do-or-die" difference between success and failure on Airbnb – especially for new hosts.

To begin, draw a simple monthly table like the one on the following page (or visit **padlifter.com/pricing-table** to download one).

MONTH	AVAILABLE LISTINGS	AVERAGE NIGHTLY COST	NEW AVERAGE NIGHTLY COST	
			NEW AVERAGE NIGHTLY COST	WITH TEMPORARY 30% REDUCTION
JAN				
FEB				
MAR				
APR				
MAY				
JUN				
JUL				
AUG				
SEP				
OCT				
NOV				
DEC				
AVERAGE:				

The next thing you'll want to do is step into the shoes of a guest that's looking to find a place on Airbnb *just like yours.*

To do so, hop onto Airbnb and do a search as if *you* were a guest trying to find a place in your neighborhood. Be as specific as possible when entering the location (for example, enter "Gramercy Park, New York" instead of just "New York").

For the dates, select check-in as the 15th January and check-out the 16th January (i.e. the middle of the month):

⌂	Gramercy Park	15 Jan – 16 Jan	1 guest

Once Airbnb display your search results, work through the different search filters presented to you (above the listing thumbnails and below the search bar at the top). Select all the filters that are applicable to your listing.

For example, if you're going to Airbnb your entire three bedroom, two bathroom apartment, then select "Entire Home" for *Room Type* and "3+ Bedrooms" and "2+ Bathrooms" for *Rooms and beds*:

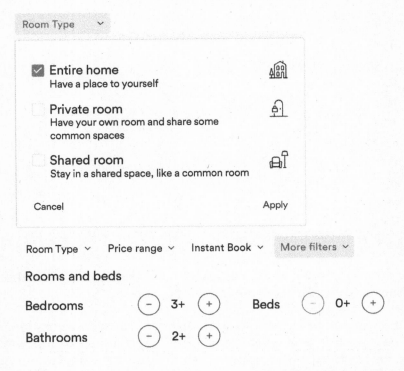

Also select any amenities, facilities or other relevant filters that help categorize your listing with other like-for-like listings.

From the results that Airbnb now present you with, there are two critical pieces of information you'll be interested in:

1. Average nightly price

Under *Price range* (the search filter at the top), Airbnb will tell you what the average nightly price is:

$10 - $1000+

The average nightly price is $891.

Cancel   Apply

In the example above, we can see that the average nightly price is *$891*. The graph also illustrates the distribution and concentration of prices across available listings.

However we can also see that this figure includes "outlier" listings on the expensive (right) end of the displayed price range graph. These expensive outlier listings are significantly more expensive than all the other listings to their left. There are also two "outlier" listings on the cheap (left) end of the price range graph too. These cheap outlier listings are significantly cheaper than all the other listings that are to their right.

We'll want to exclude outlier listings - both expensive and cheap - since they disproportionately skew the average nightly price of the neighborhood.

To do so, move the minimum price circle (on the left) to the lower end of the price range graph to exclude the *cheaper* outliers, and move the maximum price circle (on the right) to the upper end of the price range graph to exclude the *expensive* outliers:

$214 - $270

Cancel   Apply

The new average[*] nightly cost is calculated as the:
[(new minimum price) + (new maximum price)] / 2

[*] For reasons of practicality, the term "average" has been used instead of "median" for nightly cost

In the example above, the new minimum price is *$214* and the new maximum price is *$270.* The new average nightly cost is therefore ($214 + $270) / 2 = *$242.*

2. Available listings

At the very bottom of the search results page, Airbnb will tell you how many listings match your search with the filters that you specified.

In our example, Airbnb tell us that the number of available listings is 66 rentals:

1 – 18 of 66 Rentals

Do not worry about removing "outlier listings" here – it is far less important than it is to determining the average nightly price.

What do we learn from these two pieces of information? That in your local neighborhood (in the middle of January 2018), there are *66 comparable listings* to yours, and the *average nightly cost* for those listings is *$242*.

You can now populate the first two columns in the first row (i.e. for January) of your research table with those figures (ignoring the last two columns for now):

MONTH	AVAILABLE LISTINGS	AVERAGE NIGHTLY COST	NEW AVERAGE NIGHTLY COST	
			NEW AVERAGE NIGHTLY COST	WITH TEMPORARY 30% REDUCTION
JAN	66	$242		

You'll need to do this 12 times – once for each month of the year. This way, you make sure that the prices you determine account for variation across different months (this can have a big impact for locations that have wide seasonal travel fluctuations throughout the year).

To do this, simply update the dates of your search on Airbnb to the 15th of each month, and repeat for the months of February to December, repeating exactly what you have just done for January:

Once you've repeated this 11 more times, you should have a table with the first 2 columns complete. It should look something like this:

MONTH	AVAILABLE LISTINGS	AVERAGE NIGHTLY COST	NEW AVERAGE NIGHTLY COST	
			NEW AVERAGE NIGHTLY COST	WITH TEMPORARY 30% REDUCTION
JAN	66	$242		
FEB	34	$266		
MAR	64	$256		
APR	57	$271		
MAY	62	$260		
JUN	38	$243		
JUL	70	$248		
AUG	68	$239		
SEP	29	$236		
OCT	69	$232		
NOV	78	$219		
DEC	72	$215		
AVERAGE:				

It's now time to work out the **average** (*bottom row*). To do so, add the figures for each month and then divide by 12 (again, you can ignore the last two columns for now):

MONTH	AVAILABLE LISTINGS	AVERAGE NIGHTLY COST	NEW AVERAGE NIGHTLY COST	
			NEW AVERAGE NIGHTLY COST	WITH TEMPORARY 30% REDUCTION
AVERAGE:	59	$244		

Your next goal is to move away from just *understanding your competition* to determining the optimal price to charge for *your* place for each month of the year.

You may be wondering: *Why don't we just take the average nightly cost (as it exists in the current table) for each month?*

Whilst there's nothing stopping you from doing this, you ideally want to make pricing adjustments that reflect supply and demand of available listings at different times of the year: *More* available listings means more guest options, and you should therefore *charge less* (since supply is greater than demand). *Fewer* available listings means there are less guest options, and you can therefore *charge more* (since demand is greater than supply).

Whilst it's entirely up to you how much more or less you believe you should charge, a good framework to use is:

So if we use our example, the adjustments are going to look like this:

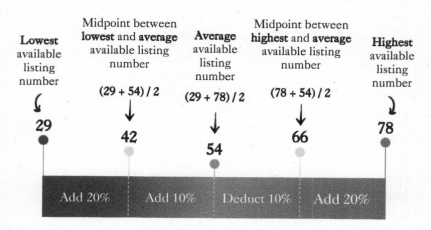

153

Or more practically...

AVAILABLE LISTINGS	PRICE CHANGE
29 – 42	Add 20%
43 – 54	Add 10%
55 – 66	Deduct 10%
67 – 78	Deduct 20%

With this information, we're now able to populate the **New Average Nightly Cost** column. Using our example, it'll look like this:

MONTH	AVAILABLE LISTINGS	AVERAGE NIGHTLY COST	NEW AVERAGE NIGHTLY COST	
			NEW AVERAGE NIGHTLY COST	WITH TEMPORARY 30% REDUCTION
JAN	66	$242	$242 – 10% = **$218**	
FEB	34	$266	$266 + 20% = **$319**	
MAR	64	$256	$256 – 10% = **$230**	
APR	57	$271	$271 – 10% = **$244**	
MAY	62	$260	$260 – 10% = **$234**	
JUN	38	$243	$243 + 20% = **$292**	
JUL	70	$248	$248 – 20% = **$198**	
AUG	68	$239	$239 – 20% = **$191**	
SEP	29	$236	$236 + 20% = **$283**	
OCT	69	$232	$232 – 20% = **$186**	
NOV	78	$219	$219 – 20% = **$175**	
DEC	72	$215	$215 – 20% = **$172**	
AVERAGE:	**59**	**$244**	**$229**	

Congratulations. You now possess a much more accurate **base nightly price** for each month of the year. Next we'll be populating the final column with strategic discounts and moving away from "one-size-fits-all" pricing...

Step 2: Moving Away From One-Size-Fits-All Pricing

Having a single, year-round price for your place almost always represents a missed opportunity. You will inevitably be over-charging or under-pricing at any given point in time.

With this step, you'll be using the information you just discovered through researching your local competition (Step 1) to make monthly adjustments to the default nightly price you currently charge year-round for your place.

If you're a new host, before updating your monthly prices, you'll also want to consider making **strategic discounts** to the figures you've just arrived at from Step 1. This is because guests are more comfortable to book with hosts that have a proven track record on Airbnb. As a new host, you have limited options for getting around this.

Offering *lower prices* to attract guests is one of the few tactics new hosts are able to use to go head-to-head with more established existing listings.

New hosts are advised to reduce their prices until a time that they've built up enough of a track-record on Airbnb to return to prices that don't need to be strategically discounted.

New hosts should discount their prices anywhere between 20-40% until they have at least 5-10 positive guest reviews. These discounts will prove a small price to pay to speed-up your success on Airbnb. The additional profits you'll subsequently make will cover (many times over) whatever short-term losses you incurred to get you there.

Assuming we applied a 30% discount to the previous example, our new temporarily-reduced figures will look like this:

MONTH	AVAILABLE LISTINGS	AVERAGE NIGHTLY COST	NEW AVERAGE NIGHTLY COST	
			NEW AVERAGE NIGHTLY COST	WITH TEMPORARY 30% REDUCTION
JAN	66	$242	$218	$218 – 30% = **$153**
FEB	34	$266	$319	$319 – 30% = **$223**
MAR	64	$256	$230	$230 – 30% = **$161**
APR	57	$271	$244	$244 – 30% = **$171**
MAY	62	$260	$234	$234 – 30% = **$164**
JUN	38	$243	$292	$292 – 30% = **$204**
JUL	70	$248	$198	$198 – 30% = **$139**
AUG	68	$239	$191	$191 – 30% = **$134**
SEP	29	$236	$283	$283 – 30% = **$198**
OCT	69	$232	$186	$186 – 30% = **$130**
NOV	78	$219	$175	$175 – 30% = **$123**
DEC	72	$215	$172	$172 – 30% = **$120**
AVERAGE:	**59**	**$244**	**$229**	**$160**

In this example we see that after applying the temporary 30% discounted rate, our new average nightly cost for the entire year is a figure of *$160*. For the month of January, it is *$153*.

If you're not using Smart Pricing, you'll want to update the pricing on your calendar to reflect these new average nightly cost figures (that include the temporary 30% reductions if you're a new host) for each month of the year.

To do so:

1. Login to Airbnb
2. In **Hosting** mode, select **Listings** from the top navigation bar
3. Select **Calendar** for your listing
4. Highlight all of the dates for the month (e.g. 1st – 31st January)

January 2018 ▾

| | Month | Year |

Mon	Tue	Wed	Thu	Fri	Sat	Sun
Jan 1	2	3	4	5	6	7
$153	$153	$153	$153	$153	$153	$153
8	9	10	11	12	13	14
$153	$153	$153	$153	$153	$153	$153
15	16	17	18	19	20	21
$153	$153	$153	$153	$153	$153	$153
22	23	24	25	26	27	28
$153	$153	$153	$153	$153	$153	$153
29	30	31				
$153	$153	$153				

5. Enter your updated nightly rate (e.g. *$153* for January) in the **Price for each night** input box

Start date	End date
01-01-2018	31-01-2018

Availability

◉ Available

○ Blocked

Price for each night

$153

Get price tips for these dates
They're based on demand and personalised for your listing.
View price tips | What do guests pay?

Add note ▾

| Cancel | Save Changes |

You're responsible for choosing the listing price.

6. Click **Save Changes**

Repeat this 11 times – once for each remaining month of the year.

Once complete, you will have successfully shifted from a one-size-fits-all pricing strategy to one that optimizes your month-by-month earning potential.

Step 3: Increasing Prices for Times of High Demand

We've just seen how it's possible to develop a more granular pricing strategy that reflects your ability to command different prices for different months of the year. You're still able to take this one step further.

There may be specific days or weeks where your city or local area is more popular than at other times throughout the year. Examples include sporting events, conferences and conventions.

Airbnb offer the ability to set **custom pricing** for these special dates.

During these times, you'll be able to charge more for your place than other times of the year. To do so, you'll need to have researched key events that are happening in your city or local area to identify *what* they are and *when* they're happening.

These events will be like honey to the bees for drawing in more tourists and travelers. And when they arrive in your city, these travelers are all going to need somewhere to stay – meaning that demand will be pushed up whilst supply (hotels, other Airbnb homes, etc.) will remain fixed.

In short, you'll be able to *charge more* for your place.

So how do you go about identifying the times when this will be possible? A basic Google search should do the trick.

Searching for something like "key events in [*your city*] [*current year*]" or "annual events in [*your city*]" should bring up a few different pages with useful information.

Below is an example for New York City:

DATE	EVENT
11 – 18 February	New York Fashion Week
17 – 28 April	Tribeca Film Festival
21 – 26 June	Gay Pride Week
9 June	Museum Mile Festival
8 – 24 August	New York International Fringe Festival
25 August – 8 September	U.S. Open
11 – 21 September	Feast of San Gennaro
6 – 9 October	New York Comic-Con
6 November	TCS New York City Marathon
27 November	Macy's Thanksgiving Day Parade

You could theoretically search for events forever, listing out every single event, both big and small, for an area as localized as your immediate neighborhood through to national holidays celebrated country-wide.

To maintain relevance, try keeping this list useful but practical by compiling a list for the **top 10-15 key events** that you believe are most likely to impact supply of short-term accommodation options for areas in and around where you live.

It's important to remember that custom weekly and monthly prices will override your normal nightly, weekly, and monthly prices; as well as any other custom nightly prices you've saved on your calendar.

If you're unsure how much more you should (or could) be charging for times of special events, a good little trick is to check out how much more hotels are charging for the same time period. You won't necessarily be copying their exact prices, but you may wish to replicate similar price pattern increases for the amounts you already regularly charge.

When it comes to custom pricing for local events like a conference or festival, it's important to become aware of these sooner rather than later and stay one step ahead of the game. Guests looking to attend these events will often try lock in their accommodation well before the actual event or its immediate run-up. If you increase your prices *after* they've already booked, you've missed the opportunity to charge more for your place.

You should aim to lock-in custom price increases for key events 6-12 months before the event actually takes place. This is why conducting event research as early as possible is so important.

Using the example from the previous table, the New York Fashion Week is happening from 11-18 February.

If we lived in New York, we may wish to increase our prices for those dates knowing that there will be a greater demand for Airbnb listings in New York that week.

Before increasing your prices for a specific event, it's important to make sure that the sort of guests likely to attend the event are guests that would actually be interested in your place. For example, if you're offering a shared room in a non-glamorous neighborhood on the outskirts of the city; a custom price increase for the New York Fashion Week probably isn't for you.

To customize your pricing for a specific (set of) night(s):

1. Login to Airbnb
2. In **Hosting** mode, select **Listings** from the top navigation bar
3. Select **Calendar** for your listing
4. Select any upcoming day or set of days

February 2018 ▾

Month Year

Mon	Tue	Wed	Thu	Fri	Sat	Sun
29	30	31	Feb 1	2	3	4
$153 5	$153 6	$153 7	$223 8	$223 9	$223 10	$223 11
$223 12	$223 13	$223 14	$223 15	$223 16	$223 17	$350 18
$350	$350	$350	$350	$350	$350	$350
$223 26	$223 27	$223 28	$161 Mar 1	$161 2	$161 3	$161 4
$161	$161	$161	$161	$161	$161	$161

5. Enter your increased nightly rate in the **Price for each night** input box

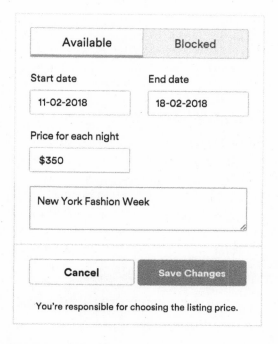

6. Click **Save Changes**

Step 4: Offering Long-Term Discounts

Airbnb provide the ability to offer long-term discounts that encourage guests to book longer reservations by offering a weekly or monthly discount.

It may seem counter-intuitive but sometimes charging less for your place on Airbnb can net you more profits than charging more.

Offering weekly or monthly discounts may be a great incentive for guests requiring a long-term accommodation option.

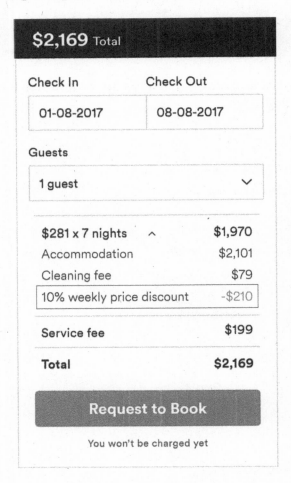

$2,169 Total

Check In	Check Out
01-08-2017	08-08-2017

Guests

1 guest ⌄

$281 x 7 nights ^	$1,970
Accommodation	$2,101
Cleaning fee	$79
10% weekly price discount	-$210
Service fee	$199
Total	**$2,169**

Request to Book

You won't be charged yet

You may lose a few dollars for each night of the booking, but potentially gain a longer-term and more lucrative guest. This is especially so when the guest is open to the idea of an extended stay.

Consider the following example scenarios – one where a weekly discount is offered, and one where no weekly discount is offered:

	SCENARIO 1: Discount Offered	SCENARIO 2: No Discount Offered
Nightly Rental Price	$100	$100
Discount for Weekly Stays or Longer	10%	None
Monthly Number of **1 night** Stays	1	1
Monthly Number of **2 night** Stays	2	2
Monthly Number of **Weekly** Stays	3	2
MONTLY INCOME:	($100 x1) + ($200 x2) + ($700 x3 - 10%) = **$2,390**	($100 x1) + ($200 x2) + ($700 x2) = **$1,900**

As you can see, when the host in Scenario 1 offers a 10% weekly discount to guests, they were able to attract **one additional weekly stay** in their place. This ended up scoring Host 1 an additional $490 in monthly revenue.

Guests are enticed by discounts, and are more likely to book places that offer them reduced rates.

As well as making your place appear cheaper than others being considered, long-term discounts also promote longer stays which have the added bonuses of optimizing your occupancy rates and lowering individual stay overheads too.

When used correctly, long-term discounting has the effect of making you a more profitable host on Airbnb.

Weekly discounts will apply to the entirety of any reservation for 7-27 nights. Monthly discounts will apply to the entirety of any reservation for 28 nights or longer. These discounts will apply even if you've set a one-time price for a specific week or month.

For any additional nights beyond a week or a month, the discount will still apply to the additional nights beyond the single week or month. For example, if you set a base nightly price of $100 and offered a 10% weekly discount, then a 9-night reservation would be calculated as 9 x ($100 – 10%). It would not be 7 x ($100 – 10%) + 2 x $100.

Guests see any long term pricing options you offer on your listing page:

Prices	Extra people: No Charge	Weekly Discount: 10%
	Cleaning Fee: $80	Monthly Discount: 20%
	Security Deposit: $500	

When they make a long-term reservation request they will see your discount in their price breakdown.

An added benefit of setting a monthly discount rate is appearing in long-term searches (of 28 nights or more), which is only possible for hosts that have offered a monthly discount.

If uncertain of how much to discount your place for long-term stays, do a search for comparable listings in your local area and look at the weekly and monthly discounts offered by these other listings (try to find "established" listings with 15+ reviews).

Airbnb also offer discounting price tips based on your listing's features and amenities, location, booking history, availability, and seasonal supply and demand in your area:

Discounts

Encourage travelers to book longer stays by offering a discount.

Weekly

Your average weekly price with a 10% discount is $1613

10 %

Tip: 17%

Monthly

Your average weekly price with a 20% discount is $6226

20 %

Tip: 31%

You can also set a custom price for a specific week or month.

Over time and with trial-and-error, you can experiment to see the impact higher and lower long-term discounts have on your bookings. When starting off, opt for larger discounts if in doubt.

To set your weekly and monthly discounts:

1. Login to Airbnb
2. In **Hosting** mode, select **Listings** from the top navigation bar
3. Select **Manage listing** for your listing
4. Click on **Pricing** from the menu at the top
5. Click the **Edit** button for the **Discounts** section
6. Enter your weekly and/or monthly discounts into the **Weekly** and **Monthly** input boxes
7. Click the **Save** button

Changes may take up to an hour to appear on your public listing page.

Step 5: Adding Extra Fees

Weekend Pricing

Airbnb allow hosts to add an extra fee for *weekends* in light of the fact that more travelers travel on these days. This means there's more demand and therefore justification for why you're able to charge more for your place.

When enabled, weekend pricing replaces your default nightly price for every *Friday* and *Saturday*.

> **Weekend pricing**
> This nightly price will replace your base price for every Friday and Saturday.
>
> $

Weekend pricing should be reserved for listings that receive an increase in travel on weekends. If your place receives travelers fairly consistently across the entire week, then the higher prices that come with implementing weekend pricing may actually serve as a disincentive for guests considering booking your place when less expensive alternative options exist.

Again, there is no prescribed figure you should use when it comes to increasing your prices for the weekend, however a 10-15% increase on your regular weekday rate is seen as a common and acceptable amount.

For a more accurate idea, conduct a search on Airbnb for listings in your area to see *if,* and *how much more,* other listings charge for weekends. Similarly, you can also search online for local hotels to see if *they* increase their prices for weekends – another good indication that it's safe for you to do so too.

Remember that it is a *dollar amount* (not percentage) that is specified for weekend pricing.

To add a weekend price to your listing:

1. Login to Airbnb
2. In **Hosting** mode, select **Listings** from the top navigation bar
3. Select **Manage listing** for your listing
4. Click on **Pricing** from the menu at the top
5. Click the **Edit** button for the **Extra charges** section
6. Enter your weekend price into the **Weekend pricing** input box
7. Click the **Save** button

Additional Guests

Hosts have the ability to charge a fee for each night of a reservation for additional guests.

You specify the amount for each additional guest, as well as define the number of guests required before the additional guest fee kicks in:

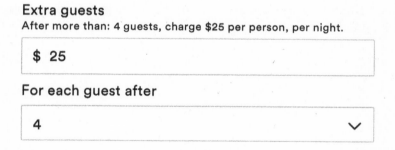

Extra guests
After more than: 4 guests, charge $25 per person, per night.

$ 25

For each guest after

4 ∨

The additional guest fee will then apply for each additional guest for each night of the booking.

The **benefit** of using the additional guest fee is that you're able to offer your place at a lower price and only charge more for bookings that actually require a higher guest count. In this way, it has the potential to make your place cheaper to smaller parties looking for a place to stay.

The **downside** of using the additional guest fee is that it is difficult to enforce in the absence of you being there at check-in to confirm the number of guests actually arriving for a booking. Some guests also interpret the fee as being indicative of an overbearing host which may serve as a disincentive for booking your home in the first place.

It is therefore important to weigh up the pros and cons of using the additional guest fee for your place. This decision inevitably involves considering who your target guests are and what kind of space you're offering on Airbnb.

In the U.S., additional guest fees typically range between $10 - $25 per night per guest.

To add an extra guest fee to your listing:

1. Login to Airbnb
2. In **Hosting** mode, select **Listings** from the top navigation bar
3. Select **Manage listing** for your listing
4. Click on **Pricing** from the menu at the top
5. Click the **Edit** button for the **Extra charges** section
6. Enter your extra guest fee into the **Extra guests** input box
7. Click the **Save** button

When (and When Not) to Lower Your Prices

It may sound counter-intuitive, but having a fully booked-out calendar on Airbnb is not always a good thing.

Guests are more likely to place bookings closer to the current date. If your place is being booked months in advance, it means that guests see your place as a *bargain* in comparison to other comparable alternatives they may also be looking at. It means that all things being equal, your place stood out because it was cheaper than the alternatives.

Whilst you've gained the security of a fully-booked calendar, under-charging can often represent an equal, if not bigger, missed opportunity than over-charging.

Let's take the following example:

	SCENARIO 1: Fully-booked, Cheaper pricing	**SCENARIO 2:** Partially-booked, More expensive
Nightly Rental Price	$75	$125
Monthly Occupancy	100%	75%
Number of Vacant Nights	0	7
Monthly Airbnb Income	(30 x 100%) x $75 = **$2,250**	(30 x 75%) x $125 = **$2,812.50**

As you can see, Host 2 still makes *$562.50* ($2,812.50 minus $2,250) more than Host 1, despite having 7 nights of empty vacancy (vs. none for Host 1).

As a general strategy, start off by locking in your target prices (i.e. the prices you believe you should *ideally* be charging for your place).

You shouldn't need to consider reducing your prices until at least one month before the current date. As you get closer to the current date, gradually begin to reduce your prices every few days as the current date approaches.

Save significant price reductions for last-minute holes in your calendar that will almost certainly remain unfilled because of other bookings that sandwich it.

As a rule of thumb, you can look to reduce your nightly rate by 10% each day in the final week leading up to a vacant block on your calendar. The proviso to this is knowing your "red line" – the amount at which it becomes unprofitable and/or not worth your time or effort to getting booked below that price.

Ensure also that any short-term bookings you do accept are not likely to compromise your ability to accept a longer, more lucrative booking.

All of this inevitably requires operating according to a framework of assumptions and educated guesses. Things won't always work out in your favor. Nonetheless, lowering your prices to fill holes in your calendar, and being strategic with the bookings you decide to accept will ultimately pay off in the long run.

Booking Settings, Calendar Management and Getting Found

Adding a Minimum Stay Requirement

Think about what's involved in having a guest come stay at your place: You need to communicate with the guest prior to their arrival. You need to organize to have the place cleaned. You need to provide access and exchange keys. All of this takes time. And time is money.

Now imagine any given month: Let's say it has 30 days. And let's say that you've hit the jackpot and miraculously have 100% occupancy. Let's assume that when you add up the time and costs involved in preparing your place for each stay, it comes to $25. And let's assume that you charge $100 per night to stay in your place.

If we play out two scenarios – one *with* and one *without* a minimum stay requirement – let's take a look at the profitability of each...

	SCENARIO 1	**SCENARIO 2**
Scenario	30x **1 night** stays	10x **3 night** stays
Income	At $100 per night and with 30 nights you receive **$3,000**	
Costs	With $25 of costs per stay and 30 stays to prepare for, you've spent **$750**	With $25 of costs per stay and 10 stays to prepare for, you've spent **$250**
Profit	$3,000 - $750 = **$2,250**	$3,000 - $250 = **$2,750**

Scenario 2 nets you $500 more profit than Scenario 1, achieved simply by implementing a minimum stay requirement.

Some naysayers will say something to the effect that implementing a minimum stay requirement will impede your ability to achieve a 100% occupancy rate, with the rationale that it's easier to fill 30x *1-night* stays than it is to fill your calendar with 10x *3-night* stays amongst multiple guests.

This is definitely true. However even if we deduct one of those 3-night stays to achieve only 90% occupancy, using the example above, we still make a profit of $2,475, which is *still* $225 more than Scenario 1 (which had no minimum stay requirement).

In summary, the specific numbers are less important than the principle – the idea that it is very often worthwhile making *small sacrifices to your occupancy rate* if that provides you with the opportunity to implement a minimum stay requirement that ultimately nets you greater profits.

The only proviso is ensuring that you keep your minimum stay requirement to something reasonable like two or three nights. Requirements bigger than this may start becoming a prohibitive factor in getting found and booked.

To set a minimum stay requirement:

1. Login to Airbnb
2. In **Hosting** mode, select **Listings** from the top navigation bar
3. Select **Manage listing** for your listing
4. Click on **Availability** from the menu at the top
5. Click the **Edit** button for the **Trip length** section
6. Enter your minimum stay requirement in the **Minimum stay** input box
7. Click the **Save** button

Here, you're able to set the minimum number of nights a guest's reservation request will need to adhere to:

Trip length

Minimum stay
2 nights

Maximum stay
nights

How long can guests stay?

Travelers can book stays of 2 nights or longer.

2 nights   No max

Setting a Minimum Stay Requirement for Seasons, Weekends and Specific Dates

You're also able to add a minimum stay requirement for specific periods of time.

If you select this option, you specify your minimum night stay requirement for either:

- Any of the four seasons (June-August, September-November, December-February, March-May)
- Reservations that include a Friday or Saturday night
- Any specific dates that you specify (e.g. periods of high demand such as the Christmas / New Year period)

You can also add a requirement that guests are only able to check-in on a **particular day of the week**.

Edit a requirement

During

Specific dates ⌄

Start date

26/07/2017

End date

25/08/2017

Minimum stay

7 nights

☑ Guests must arrive on a specific day

Check-in is on

Mondays ⌄

Mondays
Tuesdays
Wednesdays
Thursdays
Fridays
Saturdays
Sundays

Save   Cancel

These custom requirements will also display on your Airbnb listing page under **Availability**:

Availability	2 nights minimum stay. From **Jul 26 - Aug 25, 2017** the minimum stay is **7 nights**.

To add a requirement for seasons and weekends, or to limit when guests can check-in to a specific day of the week, follow the same instructions for setting a minimum stay requirement (on page 173) and click the **Add a requirement for seasons or weekends** link.

Syncing Your Calendars

If you list your space on Airbnb and other websites, you can prevent multiple guests from booking the same dates by syncing your Airbnb calendar with your other calendars.

Calendar Importing

Calendar importing allows you to automatically keep your Airbnb calendar up to date with an external calendar that supports the *iCalendar* format (filename extensions include *.ical*, *.ics*, *.ifb* and *.icalendar*), including *Google Calendar* or the calendars on *HomeAway*, *iCloud* or *VRBO*.

To import a calendar:

1. Login to Airbnb
2. In **Hosting** mode, select **Listings** from the top navigation bar
3. Select **Manage listing** for your listing
4. Click on **Availability** from the menu at the top
5. Click **Import Calendar** under the **Sync calendars** section
6. Paste your calendar's URL in the **Calendar Address (URL)** input box[*]
7. Name the calendar in the **Name Your Calendar** input box
8. Click **Import Calendar**

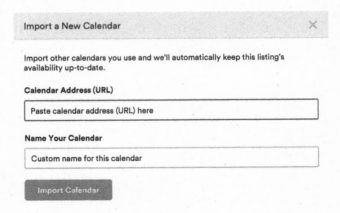

[*] For help finding your calendar's URL, read the instructions on the following page for the calendar type you wish to sync

Finding the Calendar Address (URL) of Different Calendar Types

Google Calendar

1. Find the **My calendars** section on the left, below the **Create** button
2. Hover over the calendar you want to import to Airbnb and click the down arrow
3. Select **Calendar Settings** from the dropdown menu
4. Scroll down to **Calendar Address** and select the **iCal** option
5. Copy the link and paste it into Airbnb's **Calendar Address (URL)** box

HomeAway

1. Select the listing you'd like to sync with your Airbnb calendar
2. Click **Calendar** from the left hand menu
3. Below the calendar, click **Share Your Calendar**
4. Copy the link and paste it into Airbnb's **Calendar Address (URL)** box

iCloud

1. In your iCloud account, go to **Calendar**
2. Click the radar icon next to the calendar you want to import to Airbnb
3. Check the box to make your calendar public
4. Copy the link and paste it into Airbnb's **Calendar Address (URL)** box

VRBO

1. Select the listing you'd like to sync with your Airbnb calendar
2. Click **Calendar** from the left hand menu
3. Below the calendar, click **Share Your Calendar**
4. Copy the link and paste it into Airbnb's **Calendar Address (URL)** box

If you edit an external calendar that syncs with your calendar on Airbnb, it will take a few hours for those changes to be visible to guests viewing your listing. Keep this in mind to prevent the accidental acceptance of double bookings.

Calendar Exporting

Calendar exporting lets you view your Airbnb calendar on an external calendar that supports the *iCal* format. To export your Airbnb calendar in iCal format and add it to your external calendar:

1. Login to Airbnb
2. In **Hosting** mode, select **Listings** from the top navigation bar
3. Select **Manage listing** for your listing
4. Click on **Availability** from the menu at the top
5. Click **Export Calendar** under the **Sync calendars** section
6. Copy and paste the displayed Airbnb calendar link into your iCal applications

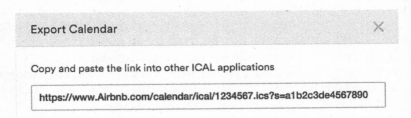

Cancellation Policies

Most guests on Airbnb that book have full intent on staying at the places that they book. Every now and then, guests will need to cancel for any number of unforeseen, but legitimate reasons. Occasionally, some guests will be frivolous in their booking, and do so with the assumption that they can always cancel their reservation at a later date.

Cancellation policies protect hosts in the event of unexpected guest cancellations. Each listing on Airbnb has a cancellation policy that is chosen by you – the host. These cancellation policies are the conditions under which you *will* or *won't* return money to a guest upon the guest choosing to cancel their reservation.

These various policies empower hosts with the level of protection they believe necessary or appropriate. The policy you decide to run with is decided entirely by you. If in doubt, hosts should err on the side of stricter cancellation policies to gain fuller protections.

Airbnb allows hosts to choose from one of three standardized cancellation policies:

	REFUND AMOUNT	NOTICE TIME REQUIRED PRIOR TO CHECK-IN*
1. Flexible	100%	1 day
2. Moderate		5 days
3. Strict	50%	7 days

* Check-in refers to your listing's local check-in time (or 3:00 PM if not specified) on day of check-in

Airbnb also provide super-strict policies offered by invitation only (e.g. to high-end resort listings) as well as long-term cancellation policies (discussed shortly) that apply to all reservations of 28 nights or more.

The cancellation policy you choose will not display until a guest views your Airbnb listing page – another reason Airbnb hosts are encouraged to opt for stricter cancellation policies.

The flip-side of this however, is that once on your listing page, Airbnb *will* inform prospective guests of cancellation policies that are favorable and attractive to them:

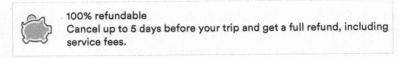

100% refundable
Cancel up to 5 days before your trip and get a full refund, including service fees.

Airbnb also offer guests a "fully refundable" search filter (i.e. for Flexible or Moderate cancellation policies) that they're able to select:

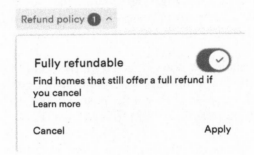

Lenient cancellation policies naturally encourage more bookings.

Guests will also be asked to agree to the host's cancellation policy when they make a booking. A host will be able to see the number of reservations a guest has cancelled over the previous 12 months when the guest submits a request to book.

Updating Your Cancellation Policy

To view or change your cancellation policy:

1. Login to Airbnb
2. In **Hosting** mode, select **Listings** from the top navigation bar
3. Select **Manage listing** for your listing
4. Click on **Booking settings** from the menu at the top
5. Click the **Edit** button for the **Policies** section
6. Choose between **Flexible**, **Moderate** or **Strict** under **Cancellation policy**
7. Click the **Save** button

Cancellation policy

Choose your policy for trip cancellations by guests. View the full details for these cancellation policies.

Flexible
Full refund 1 day prior to arrival

Moderate
Full refund 5 days prior to arrival

Strict
50% refund up until 1 week prior to arrival

If you update your cancellation policy, it will only apply to reservations that are made *after* you make the changes. It will not apply to upcoming reservations that you have already accepted.

When is a Reservation Cancelled?

A reservation is officially cancelled when the guest clicks the cancellation button on the cancellation confirmation page.

If your guest cancels a reservation in his or her Airbnb account, you will be automatically notified via email:

⚬ airbnb

Hi Thomas,

We regret to inform you that your guest Danielle cancelled reservation ABC123 starting on 2016-01-01. Per your cancellation policy, your payout has been updated to $500. Your guest was refunded $650.

An adjustment of -$630 has been applied to your account.

For more information on cancellation payouts, please see our FAQ.

Your calendar has also been updated to show that the previously booked dates are now available.

Regards,
The Airbnb Team

P.S. We know getting a cancellation is disappointing. But bookings rarely get cancelled, so don't worry, no matter how often you host, this isn't likely to happen often!

Your calendar will be automatically opened so you can again accept reservation requests from other guests for the previously-booked dates.

You can always verify the status of a reservation by logging into Airbnb and from your **Hosting** dashboard, clicking on **View all reservations** under **Reservations**. Cancelled reservations will have their **Status** listed as "**Cancelled**":

Status	Dates and Location	Guest	Details
Upcoming Reservations			
Cancelled	Jan 1-03, 2016 Family-friendly Dream NYC Apartment 100 3rd Avenue, Apt 10 Gramercy, NY 10010	Danielle S	$1000 USD total Message History Issue Refund

Payouts for cancelled reservations are not released early.

No-Shows and Cancellations After Check-In

Should your guest decide not to show up, Airbnb will uphold your cancellation policy. Your payout will be released 24 hours after the originally-scheduled check-in date (as long as you've upheld your host obligations).

This is what happens if the guest **fails to meet their pre-trip required notice obligations**:

	1ST NIGHT OF RESERVATION	REMAINING NIGHT(S) OF RESERVATION
Flexible	Non-refundable	100% refund
Moderate		50% refund
Strict		Non-refundable

If your guest has already checked in and wishes to cancel their reservation, they must vacate your place upon submitting an official cancellation.

This is what happens if the guest **chooses to leave early**:

	NIGHTS REFUNDED	REFUND AMOUNT
Flexible	All nights falling 24hrs after cancellation	100%
Moderate		50%
Strict	Non-refundable	

You have until 48 hours after the original check-out date to make any security deposit claims.

Long-Term Bookings and Cancellations

If the guest makes a long term reservation and decides to cancel the reservation before the start date, the first month of the reservation is paid to the host in full and not refunded to the guest. If the guest books a reservation and decides to cancel remaining days of the reservation midway throughout their stay, the guest must use the booking alteration tool in order to agree to a new checkout date with their host.

Regardless of the checkout date chosen, the guest is required to pay the host for the 30 days following the cancellation date, or up to the end date of the guest's original reservation if the remaining portion of the original reservation is less than 30 days.

Fee Refunds

Cleaning fees are always refunded if the guest did not check in. Service fees will be refunded through an adjustment to the final reservation total you're paid after the refund. Applicable taxes will also be retained and remitted by Airbnb.

You can always verify payouts of fee refunds in your Transaction History by logging into Airbnb and going to **Transaction History**. The updated amount you are to be paid (post-cancellation) will be stated. Note however, there will be no mention of the cancellation within the transaction history – only the updated amount that Airbnb *will* pay or *has* paid you in the form of a fee refund (as per your cancellation policy).

Cancellation Policy Examples

Flexible

1 day prior	Check-in	Check-out
Thu, Jan 26 | 3:00 PM	Fri, Jan 27 | 3:00 PM	Mon, Jan 30 | 11:00 AM
For a full refund of accommodation fees, cancellation must be made a full 24 hours prior to listing's local check in time (or 3:00 PM if not specified) on the day of check in. For example, if check-in is on Friday, the guest must cancel by Thursday of that week before check-in time.	If the guest cancels less than 24 hours before check-in, the first night is non-refundable.	If the guest arrives and decides to leave early, the accommodation fees for the nights not spent 24 hours after the official cancellation are fully refunded.

Moderate

5 days prior	Check-in	Check-out
Sun, Jan 22 | 3:00 PM	Fri, Jan 27 | 3:00 PM	Mon, Jan 30 | 11:00 AM
For a full refund of accommodation fees, cancellation must be made five full days prior to listing's local check in time (or 3:00 PM if not specified) on the day of check in. For example, if check-in is on Friday, the guest must cancel by the previous Sunday before check-in time.	If the guest cancels less than 5 days in advance, the first night is non-refundable but 50% of the accommodation fees for remaining nights will be refunded.	If the guest arrives and decides to leave early, 50% of the accommodation fees for the nights not spent 24 hours after the cancellation occurs are refunded.

Strict

7 days prior	Check-in	Check-out
Fri, Jan 20 | 3:00 PM	Fri, Jan 27 | 3:00 PM	Mon, Jan 30 | 11:00 AM
For a 50% refund of accommodation fees, cancellation must be made seven full days prior to listing's local check-in time (or 3:00 PM if not specified) on the day of check-in, otherwise no refund. For example, if check-in is on Friday, the guest must cancel by Friday of the previous week before check-in time.	If the guest cancels less than 7 days in advance, the nights not spent are not refunded.	If the guest arrives and decides to leave early, the nights not spent are not refunded.

Circumstances Where Your Cancellation Policy Won't Apply

Extenuating Circumstances

Airbnb reserve the right to not uphold your listing's cancellation policy if there are extenuating circumstances. Extenuating circumstances include:

- The **unexpected death** or **serious illness** of a guest or their immediate family member
- A **serious injury** that directly restricts a guest's ability to travel
- A **significant natural disaster** or **severe weather incidents** impacting your location or the location of the guest's departure
- **Urgent travel restrictions** or **severe security advisories** issued after the time of booking by an appropriate national or international authority (such as a government office or department)
- **Endemic disease** declared by a credible national or international authority (such as the U.S. Center for Disease Control or the World Health Organization)
- **Government-mandated obligations** issued after the time of booking

The cancellation policy will also not apply where there are legitimate safety concerns held by the guest.

Guest Refund Policy

The Airbnb Guest Refund Policy protects guests from last-minute host cancellations, lock-outs, and listings that are misrepresented, unsanitary, or lacking in promised amenities or items.

You cancellation policy may not apply if you violate one or more of Airbnb's hosting standards. These include things like communication, check-in, accuracy, cleanliness, the overall experience or maintaining an up-to-date calendar.

In the event of a complaint from a guest, notice must be given to Airbnb within 24 hours of their check-in. Airbnb will then mediate where necessary, and will have the final say in all disputes.

Issuing Additional Refunds

At the time of cancellation, your guest is automatically refunded according to your cancellation policy. Whilst you are under no obligation, if you'd like to offer your guest a bigger refund, there are two ways of doing so.

With both methods, the refund is considered final and you are not entitled to a return of any moneys you decide to refund. To ask your guest for any money back, you would need to submit a new refund request using the Airbnb Resolution Center.

Method 1: Issue Refund Button

If your guest cancelled the reservation before the check-in date, an **Issue Refund** link will appear under the reservation in the **Your Reservations** section of your Airbnb account.

The amount you are able to refund the guest will be capped by the amount that you were (or will be) paid out by Airbnb for the original booking as per your cancellation policy.

Issue Refund

The guest cancelled the reservation before checking in. Would you like to waive the cancellation policy and issue the guest a refund?

Amount $

1761

($1761 maximum)

You will not receive a full payout for this reservation. The guest will receive an email confirmation.

Cancel   Issue Refund

Method 2: Resolution Center

You can also refund your guest using the Airbnb Resolution Center (**www.airbnb.com/resolutions**). There will be a "Send or Request Money" button that is displayed upon the completion of a guest's trip which will also take you directly to the Resolution Center:

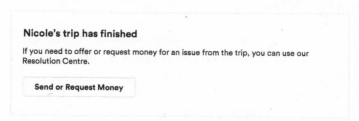

Once in the Resolution Center, select the **Send Money** button then select the relevant reservation from the list of reservations that are displayed. If the reservation you're looking for isn't in the drop-down menu, that means it's more than 60 days old and is not eligible for a Resolution Center refund.

Enter the desired amount and a message to your guest. After you send the message, your guest will be automatically notified by the Airbnb messaging system, and they have the choice of whether or not to accept the offer.

Airbnb will be automatically notified once an offer to send money has been accepted and will process the refund within 48 hours. You will be notified via email once the refund is complete.

Cancelling as a Host

There may also be rare times that you, as the *host*, need to cancel a reservation. Hosts need to be aware that despite being able to do so, there are consequences to cancelling a guest's reservation. In the event that you need to cancel a reservation, you should be familiar with the options for mitigating these consequences on your ongoing Airbnb success.

If you need to cancel a guest's reservation you have two ways of doing so:

1. On a **desktop computer:** Login to Airbnb and go to *Your Reservations*, find the reservation you need to cancel and select "*Change or Cancel*"
2. On the **Airbnb smartphone app:** Go to the *Calendar* tab on the mobile app, find and load the reservation you need to cancel, scroll down to the bottom and select "*Cancel Reservation*"

Penalties

Because cancellations can have serious implications on a guest's trip, Airbnb impose penalties on hosts that cancel confirmed reservations. These penalties include:

Cancellation Fee: Hosts that cancel any reservation within 7 days of check-in are charged a $100 cancellation fee, or a $50 cancellation fee for cancellations more than 7 days before check-in. Cancellation fees are waived for your first cancellation within a six month period. Airbnb will automatically deduct any applicable cancellation fees from your next payout.

Automated review: An automated review will be posted to the host's profile indicating that they cancelled one of their reservations. Airbnb encourage these hosts to publicly respond to clarify why they needed to cancel (which hosts have the option of doing).

Unavailable / Blocked calendar: The host's calendar will stay blocked and won't be able to accept another booking for the same dates of the cancelled reservation.

Loss of eligibility for Superhost Status: These hosts won't be eligible to earn Superhost status for one year following the most recent cancellation.

Cancellations When Using Instant Book

Hosts who use Instant Book (listings that don't require approval from the host before guests can book them) can cancel up to 3 times, penalty-free **if the host has concerns with a guest's behavior** before or during a booked trip.

Hosts using Instant Book that need to cancel must do so within 24 hours of check-in using the following steps:

1. Login to Airbnb
2. In **Hosting** mode, scroll down to **Reservations** on your hosting dashboard and select **View all reservations**
3. Find the reservation you need to cancel
4. Select **Change or Cancel**
5. Select **Cancel Reservation**
6. Select **"I'm uncomfortable with the guest's behavior"**
7. Provide a reason for why you are uncomfortable with the guest's behavior

Once you've completed those steps, your host penalties will automatically be waived and Airbnb will help your guest find another place to stay for their trip.

You can only use an Instant Book cancellation 3 times in one year and only for reservations that were made through Instant Book. Calendar inaccuracy, confusion about pricing or availability, and extenuating circumstances will not be covered by this policy.

Getting Found More Often

Having the perfect listing, being the perfect host and having the perfect place amount to nothing if no one knows you exist.

Airbnb will display listings in search results that meet a guest's specified criteria. Guests looking for a place to stay are required at minimum to provide a destination for where they wish to travel. Most guests will also enter travel dates, and many will also enter additional search criteria like room type, price range, home size and amenities.

Airbnb will display 18 listings per page, and a maximum of 17 pages (i.e. a maximum of 306 listings). This means that in big cities with lots of Airbnb listings, many places that meet a guest's search criteria won't even be displayed to a prospective guest.

Listings that do not appear on the first couple of pages of search results have little chance of being booked. The deeper your listing appears within the search results, the less likely you are to be seen by prospective guests.

Whilst the specific search algorithm used by Airbnb in determining listing placement remains unknown, there are a number of things that *are* known to assist with getting found more often:

- **Instant Book:** The ability for guests to book a listing immediately without prior host approval
- **Business Travel Ready:** Listings that specifically cater to the needs and wants of business travelers
- **Superhost Status:** Possessing a proven track record of experience in hosting and hospitality on Airbnb
- **Additional tips and tricks:** Little things you're able to do to get found more often in search results

Each of these is covered in the following sections.

Instant Book

Instant Book is a booking setting that lets guests who meet your requirements **automatically** book your space. If you enable the Instant Book setting, guests do not require your approval before they're able to book a stay at your place.

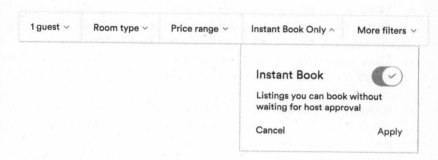

Airbnb's Instant Book feature was introduced in an effort to provide a more seamless, hassle-free booking experience for guests looking to replicate the ease of booking a hotel room quickly and simply.

For this reason, Airbnb prioritize and promote Instant Book listings to prospective guests. As an example, the following popups and notifications appear to guests when trying to book a place on Airbnb:

Since by default many hosts have a natural preference for actively vetting the guests that stay in their homes, Airbnb needed to ensure that hosts saw the value in utilizing the feature to get them on-board. Instant Book provides the following benefits to Airbnb hosts:

- **Convenience:** Allows you to book guests without needing to respond to each request.
- **More guest interest:** Guests can filter to search only for *Instant Book* listings. Instant Book listings are more popular with guests since they're able to more seamlessly plan their trip.
- **Earn more reviews:** More bookings equals more opportunities to get reviewed. And more reviews equals increased credibility and value.
- **Search placement:** Airbnb give priority placement to *Instant Book* listings in search results. It also positively affects your response rate, which will also improve your listing's placement in search results.
- **Gaining Superhost status:** Instant Book can help you reach Superhost status by maintaining a high response rate – one of the requirements for becoming an Airbnb Superhost.
- **Reduced management costs:** Your time is money. Instant Book significantly reduces the amount of time you need to invest in communicating with guests prior to bookings, translating into increased profitability for you.

Before being able to use Instant Book, Airbnb require the following from every guest looking to utilize the feature:

- A confirmed email address
- A confirmed phone number
- A profile photo
- Explanation of their trip purpose
- Information on the number of people coming on the trip
- Agreement to your house rules
- Payment information

Below is an example of information guests are required to provide before making an Instant Book reservation:

1. About Your Trip   Personal travel

Who's coming?

| 1 guest | ⌄ |

When do you think you'll check in?
To book now, check-in between 11AM – 6PM

| 4PM – 6PM | ▾ |

What's the main purpose of this trip? ⑦

⦿ Personal travel   ◯ Business travel

Say hello to your host and tell them why you're coming:

> Visiting family or friends? Seeing the sights? This helps your host plan for your trip.

You have the option of adding additional requirements, which include also requiring guests to have provided Airbnb with a government-issued ID and/or endorsements from other Airbnb hosts.

To activate Instant Book settings at any time:
1. Login to Airbnb
2. In **Hosting** mode, select **Listings** from the top navigation bar
3. Select **Manage listing** for your listing
4. Click on **Booking settings** from the menu at the top
5. Select **Guests who meet all your requirements can book without requesting approval** under **How guests can book**

How guests can book

Hosts often get double the reservations when they let guests book without requiring approval. Learn more

○ Guests who meet all your requirements can book without requesting approval

RECOMMENDED

Everyone else must send a reservation request

○ All guests must send reservation requests

Instant Book will apply to all available dates on your calendar. Once Instant Book has been activated, you'll see the Instant Book lightning bolt icon on your *Manage Listings* page:

Despite all of its benefits, Instant Book is not without its risks or complications. It is also not always advisable for hosts with limited experience on Airbnb. Before deciding to activate Instant Book, ensure that you understand the risks involved and follow simple steps to mitigate those risks.

The most effective strategy is simply communicating as much information about your listing and expectations upfront through a detailed listing that eliminates surprises for any prospective guests.

If you decide to activate Instant Book, monitor your profitability and time investment both before and after having activated it. Ensure that the feature *helps*, not hinders, your investments in Airbnb; and make decisions around its continued use accordingly.

The following pages detail some of the risks and recommendations for mitigating those risks, associated with the Instant Book feature.

Risks and Key Considerations

Making Mistakes

The Risk:

Since the Instant Book feature entails automating many of the interactions, communications and processes that would otherwise take place between a host and guest, **newer hosts risk making mistakes through the automation of processes and communications that would otherwise be happening manually and in person.**

They will also **miss out on a number of key learnings** that will be useful for their ongoing Airbnb education.

Recommendation:

Not for newbies. If new to Airbnb or still trying to learn the ropes, save use of the Instant Book feature till a time that you've familiarized yourself with the ins-and-outs of the Airbnb booking and hosting processes.

Calendar Inaccuracies

The Risk:

Since reservations are automated, they rely on an up-to-date and accurate calendar. Some hosts list their property on multiple vacation rental sites. These hosts don't necessarily automatically sync their Airbnb calendars, or may not have updated their calendars to reflect their property's true availability.

When double-bookings or calendar syncing mistakes are made, Instant Book **may result in the need to cancel reservations you realize you're unable to accommodate.**

Recommendation:

Maintain an up-to-date calendar. Ensure that you sync your Airbnb calendar with all other vacation rental websites you list on. Update your Airbnb calendar to reflect your true availability, including blocking out any dates that your place is unavailable.

Impacts to Occupancy Rate

The Risk:

Activating Instant Book inevitably means losing a degree of control over your calendar and the bookings you strategically choose to accept or decline to optimize your occupancy rates.

Guests have the ability to make reservations that may **create undesirable gaps to your calendar and which prove difficult to fill.** All of this negatively impacts your occupancy rate.

Recommendation:

Increase your minimum stay requirement. Increasing your minimum stay requirement will ensure that potential guests don't have the ability to meaningfully disrupt your occupancy rate or profitability with a standalone short stay reservation that prevents other longer and more profitable reservations from taking place.

Concerns About Instant Book Guests

The Risk:

With the ability for guests to use the Instant Book feature to book a stay at your place without pre-approval, hosts **lose the ability to screen out potentially undesirable guests** they would otherwise not accept to host.

Recommendation:

Cancelling reservations without penalty. Hosts who use Instant Book can cancel up to 3 times penalty-free if they have concerns with a guest's behavior before or during their trip.

These cancellations are valid only for reservations that were booked through Instant Book (they do not include calendar inaccuracy, confusion about pricing or availability, or extenuating circumstances).

Also consider **adding additional requirements** such as requiring guests to have provided Airbnb with a government-issued ID and/or endorsements from other Airbnb hosts.

Business Travel Ready

There are a few perks of having your listing marked as "Business Travel Ready". This title enables you to highlight your listing by displaying a badge (💼) that assists business travelers to find it easily.

Guests looking for a place to stay on Airbnb also have the ability to filter their searches to only display listings that are marked as possessing amenities for work trips:

Room Type ⌄   Price range ⌄   Instant Book ⌄   More filters ⌄

Travelling for work?

Business Travel Ready   (✕)
Show homes with amenities for work trips like wifi and 24-hour check-in.

When your listing is marked as "Business Travel Ready", you're able to get more reservations with access to bookings from thousands of professionals who use Airbnb. You're also able to fill up empty dates since business travelers often book mid-week and during slow seasons.

For your listing to be classified as "Business Travel Ready" you need to meet the following criteria:

Entire Place: Room type must be *Entire Place* (as opposed to a *Private* or *Shared Room*), and the space must be an eligible property type (e.g. no treehouses, lighthouses, etc.).

Experience: Listings must have at least 3 reviews (i.e. prior bookings).

Responsiveness: Hosts must have responded to 90% of reservation requests within 24 hours over the last year:

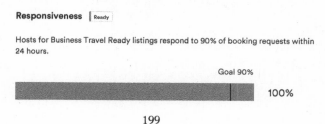

Responsiveness | Ready |

Hosts for Business Travel Ready listings respond to 90% of booking requests within 24 hours.

Goal 90%

100%

Business Amenities: The space must have the following amenities:

- ☑ Essentials
  Towels, bed sheets, soap, and toilet paper
- ☑ Shampoo
- ☑ Wireless Internet
  Continuous access in the listing
- ☑ Hangers
- ☑ Iron
- ☑ Hair dryer

- ☑ Laptop friendly workspace
  A table or desk with space for a laptop and a chair that's comfortable to work in
- ☑ Smoke detector
- ☑ Carbon monoxide detector
- ☑ No Smoking Allowed
- ☑ No Pets Live on This Property

Self Check-In: Business travelers must be able to check-in anytime on their own via any of the following methods:

- Smart lock – a lock on the door that guests can open with a keypad or mobile app
- Keypad – guests can open the door with a code
- Lockbox – a key safe that guests can open with a code
- Doorman – someone that's available 24 hours a day to let guests in

5-Star Reviews: Listings must have 5-stars for at least 60% of primary, cleanliness and accuracy reviews:

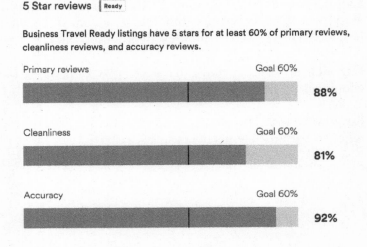

5 Star reviews | Ready |

Business Travel Ready listings have 5 stars for at least 60% of primary reviews, cleanliness reviews, and accuracy reviews.

Primary reviews — Goal 60% — **88%**

Cleanliness — Goal 60% — **81%**

Accuracy — Goal 60% — **92%**

Commitment: Hosts mustn't have cancelled confirmed reservations within 7 days of the check-in date. If a listing has a cancellation within 7 days of a confirmed check-in date, it won't be considered for Business Travel Ready for 1 year from the cancellation date.

To review your listing's "Business Travel Ready" eligibility status:

1. Login to Airbnb
2. In **Hosting** mode, select **Listings** from the top navigation bar
3. Select **Manage listing** for your listing
4. Click on **Listing details** from the menu at the top

If your place *is* recognized as "Business Travel Ready", Airbnb will display a **Business Travel** section, stating that "This listing has essential business travel amenities":

Business Travel

📼 This listing has essential business travel amenities.

If your place is *not* recognized as "Business Travel Ready", Airbnb will display a **Make your space Business Travel Ready** link under **Amenities**:

Amenities

| 🛋 Essentials | ☝ Hair dryer |
| 🍴 Kitchen | 👔 Hangers |

Make your space Business Travel Ready

Qualification is automatically evaluated based on information a host provides about their listing, the reviews for that listing, the host's prior cancellation history for confirmed reservations, and the responsiveness of the host to prior reservation requests. In evaluating the host's responsiveness, Airbnb will consider data from the preceding 12 months.

Listings are evaluated for business travel readiness on a rolling basis. There is no application process to be considered for eligibility. Eligibility is automatically evaluated on a regular schedule determined by Airbnb. You and your listing need to continue to qualify after the initial evaluation in order to maintain Business Travel Ready status.

Superhost Status

Superhosts are experienced Airbnb hosts who provide a shining example for other hosts, and extraordinary hospitality and experiences for their guests.

Once a host reaches Superhost status, the Superhost badge will automatically appear on their profile and listing to help guests identify them:

In the eyes of prospective guests, being a Superhost will position you as a better host than other hosts that lack the coveted title. You are therefore likely to receive more reservation requests as a result of having earned the badge.

Guests are also able to filter their search results to only display listings of Superhosts. In this way, Superhosts have an additional advantage for getting found and booked over those that are not Superhosts.

To become a Superhost, you need to have an Airbnb account in good standing, and need to have met the following 4 requirements over the past year:

Requirement 1: Hosting Experience

Superhosts must have **hosted 10 trips within the last year.**

This requirement is assessed quarterly. At every quarterly review, Superhosts need to have hosted 10 trips in the last 12 months prior to the review date.

If attaining Superhost Status is important to you, you may feel compelled to make ad-hoc compromises to reservation requests that you would otherwise have rejected in the lead-up to assessment review dates (overviewed shortly).

Furthermore, not all hosts live in places where meeting this requirement is easy, let alone possible.

Aspiring Superhosts may consider reducing or eliminating minimum night booking requirements or lowering their prices to attract bookings that would otherwise not come through.

If every quarter is a "race to the finish-line", then these compromises and last minute efforts may be more hassle than they're worth. If that's the case, Superhost status may not be for you.

Requirement 2: High Response Rate

Superhosts must maintain a **90% response rate or higher**.

Your Superhost response rate is calculated on the responses you send within 24 hours to the booking inquiries and requests you've received over the past 365 days.

If attaining Superhost status is important to you, ensure that you respond to all booking inquiries and requests within 24 hours.

The easiest way to prevent messages falling through the cracks and responding to them promptly is by activating text message push notifications or receiving push notifications straight to your smartphone if you've downloaded the Airbnb mobile app.

All Airbnb hosts should aspire to respond promptly to guest inquiries and reservation requests out of courtesy and respect. However, maintaining a 90% response rate may not be practical to many hosts for a variety of reasons.

If a near-perfect response rate sounds unrealistic, you may wish to consider whether aspiring for Superhost status is right for you.

Requirement 3: 5-Star Reviews

At least **80% of a Superhost's reviews** need to be **5-stars**.

This refers to the *primary* reviews you've received from guests (not the individual category reviews). This can be found in the *Stats > Host Standards* section of your Airbnb dashboard. If a host receives anything less than a 5-star rating for any of the core Airbnb category review criteria (accuracy, cleanliness, check-in, communication, location and value) then the review isn't an overall 5-star review and won't count towards the 80% threshold.

If attaining Superhost status is important to you, then the best thing you can do is to continue providing phenomenal guest experiences and openly communicating with your guests on the importance of positive reviews for your ongoing Airbnb success.

So long as your guest had a problem-free stay, it always helps to promptly review them ASAP after their stay. They will receive a notification that you've reviewed them, which should give them a "gentle nudge" to then do the same for you. If they want to read what you wrote about them without waiting out the 14-day review period, they'll need to submit their review of you.

Strategies for winning 5-star reviews from guests is covered in greater detail on page 295 in the *Building Trust and Getting 5-Star Reviews* chapter.

Unfortunately, unreasonably negative guest reviews do still happen on Airbnb. Not only that, it is also something that's almost entirely outside of your control. Some guests will have unrealistic expectations and some guests will work to an unreasonable rating scale. Both of these factors may adversely impact the reviews guests like these will leave you.

Furthermore, if you've received 5-star reviews 80% of the time or more, but fewer than half your guests have actually left you a review, you won't receive Superhost status. To this extent, an element of becoming an Airbnb Superhost unfortunately remains outside of your direct control.

Requirement 4: Commitment

Superhosts **don't cancel confirmed reservations.**

It may seem obvious, but cancelling a guest's reservation can have serious implications on their trip. Cancellations you make under extenuating circumstances won't count against your Superhost status, but all other cancellations will.

Extenuating circumstance cases will be contingent on proper documentation, where valid. Airbnb won't mark legitimate cancellations as "made under extenuating circumstances" unless they're reported to them within two weeks of the cancellation. Therefore ensure that you inform Airbnb of any cancellations and the extenuating circumstances that caused them ASAP.

If attaining Superhost status is important to you, ensure that you are prepared to sign-up for honoring all confirmed reservations you've accepted. Anything less is a good indication that Superhost status might not be for you.

The Process for Becoming a Superhost

You do not need to apply to become a Superhost. The Superhost requirements are measured every 3 months, and are based on your activity over the past year.

The assessment dates are the first of the month in January, April, July, and October.

Throughout the quarters, Airbnb will provide you with updates on your Superhost status and upcoming assessment dates:

Unlock Superhost

Next assessment: **1 Apr 2017**

You're not meeting requirements for Superhost status—we hope you will soon! These requirements are measured every 3 months.

View details

Almost a Superhost

Next assessment: **1 Apr 2017**

If you continue to meet requirements, you'll receive Superhost status after the next assessment.

View details

Pending assessment

Assessment ends: **14 Apr 2017**

We'll let you know if you've received Superhost status after the assessment period has ended.

Learn more

You're a Superhost

Next assessment: **1 Jul 2017**

If you continue to meet requirements, you'll keep your Superhost status after the next assessment

View details

The process is automated, which means that Airbnb can't update your status in-between assessment dates. If you meet the program requirements on any relevant assessment date, you'll *automatically* qualify for Superhost status.

Airbnb will notify you of your Superhost status at the end of each assessment period – usually within 2 weeks after the assessment begins:

Thomas, it's time to celebrate. You've earned Superhost status!

You've delighted your guests, and we think that deserves to be rewarded. In the year leading up to 2017-04-01, you hosted 18 trips, earned 5-star reviews 83% of the time, and had a 100% response rate with no cancellations.

We've developed the Superhost program to celebrate and support responsive, active and highly-rated hosts like you. Here are some of the great benefits:

Priority support: We move Superhost calls to the front of the phone queue. To get in touch fast, call (+)1 855 424 7262 or tweet at @AirbnbHelp.

Stand out in Search: Guests can easily find recognised hosts like you when they use the Superhost search filter.

Superhost badge: Everyone on Airbnb can see this special badge, and you can embed it on other websites or on social media. Go ahead – show off a little. #superhost

Your status is reevaluated each quarter, so remember to keep an eye on your host dashboard, and keep up the fabulous hospitality!

The Airbnb Team

Learn More

Superhost Terms & Conditions

Hosts who have had their Superhost status revoked may regain their Superhost status during a future qualification period if they again meet the qualification requirements for the most recent previous 12 months on that review date. It may take a couple days for your Superhost badge to appear on your listing.

You're always able to check your progress in meeting the Superhost criteria as well as the next assessment date. To do so:

1. Login to Airbnb
2. In **Hosting** mode, select **Stats** from the top navigation bar
3. Select **Standards** from the sub-menu bar beneath the main menu bar

Hosting Standards

Commitment rate

100%

You've cancelled 0 reservations in the past 365 days. Staying committed to reservations helps guests travel with peace of mind. Keep it up!

Response rate

100%

You've responded to 10 of the last 10 enquiries and requests. Guests love quick responses. Keep it up!

Overall rating

4.8

This takes into account all your reviews from the past 365 days. Nice work!

Superhost requirements

Your current progress towards the upcoming assessment is based on the following date range:

Select date range

1 Jul 2016 – 30 Jun 2017 (Current)

	Superhost	You
Completed trips	10	28
Commitment rate	100%	100%
Response rate	90%	100%
5-star trips	80%	88%
Review rate	50%	96%

Additional Tips and Tricks for Getting Found More Often

Whilst Airbnb hosts would like nothing more than a magic wand to wave for getting found more often, it unfortunately does not exist. There are however a few specific things that hosts are able to keep up their sleeves for increasing the likelihood of getting found in search results.

Below are 10 additional tips and tricks you can implement to help your listing get found more often on Airbnb:

Relevance to Search Factors

Ensure that you provide Airbnb with as much information about your place as possible. Airbnb will try to match any search filters specified by guests, to listings that best line up with what those guests are looking for.

The easiest way to score a quick win here is simply by specifying as many of the amenities you provide at your place on your Airbnb listing:

Pets allowed

Free parking on premises

Lift in building

Family/kid friendly

Internet

Doorman

Suitable for events

Gym

Kitchen

Breakfast

Buzzer/wireless intercom

Air conditioning

Laptop friendly workspace

Iron

Hair dryer

Smoking allowed

Wheelchair accessible

Wireless Internet

Indoor fireplace

Cable TV

Spa

Pool

Dryer

Hangers

Shampoo

Washer

Essentials

TV

Heating

Private entrance

Responsiveness to Reservation Requests

Airbnb look favorably upon hosts that respond quickly to reservation requests as it demonstrates a commitment to the Airbnb community.

Airbnb presume that these good habits will likely continue throughout a guest's stay and will reward hosts they think will provide guests with superior experiences.

The importance of remaining responsive is covered in greater detail on page 229 in the *Booking Acceptance and Communicating with Guests* chapter.

Booking Acceptance

The flip-side of remaining responsive is a continual pattern of rejecting reservation requests. This demonstrates a *lack* of commitment to the Airbnb community.

Whilst inevitably hosts will reject reservation requests for a whole variety of reasons, a consistent pattern of declining reservation requests will be frowned upon by Airbnb.

Airbnb favor hosts that they believe are more committed to accommodating guests, and will display listings from these hosts higher up in search results.

Previous Bookings

Airbnb assume that a host with a long track record of hosting will naturally be a better host than a new host still learning their way around the Airbnb ecosystem. To ensure optimal guest experiences, Airbnb will favor hosts that have been hosting on Airbnb for longer and whom possess a solid track record of reviews.

Do everything in your power to maximize the number of bookings you receive as quickly as possible. Whilst largely outside the direct control of a host, one way for new hosts to do this is to…

Reduce Your Pricing

When starting off on Airbnb, you'll want to reduce your regular prices anywhere from 20-40% for your first few bookings. Once you've hosted 5-10 bookings and have a few positive reviews against your name, you're no longer the "new kid on the block" and you'll be able to boost your prices back to normal.

Maintain 5-Star Reviews

Airbnb naturally want to link guests with hosts that will create the best possible experiences for their customers. The more your reviews suggest that you are the type of host likely to provide a 5-star experience, the more likely Airbnb will be in wanting to promote you to guests looking for a place to stay.

122 Reviews	★★★★★		
Accuracy	★★★★★	Location	★★★★★
Communication	★★★★★	Check In	★★★★★
Cleanliness	★★★★★	Value	★★★★★

If you're a new host, it's worth under-charging and over-delivering to get some "quick wins" on the board.

Getting 5-star reviews is covered in greater depth on page 295 in the *Building Trust and Getting 5-Star Reviews* chapter.

Use Professional, High-Quality Photos

Ensure the photos you display are professional high-quality photos, and that you showcase no less than 10 photos of your place on your listing.

Airbnb naturally favor listings that enable guests to envisage what it would be like to stay in a place, and there's no easier way of doing that than with photos that show off your place in its best light.

Demonstrate Your Trustworthiness and Reliability

Airbnb want guests to feel instant comfort with the hosts they're considering staying with. Providing multiple forms of verified ID (connecting your Airbnb profile to social networks, uploading official ID and confirming personal details) will assist Airbnb in portraying you as a reliable and trustworthy host from the instant a guest considers staying at your place.

Airbnb will prioritize hosts that have multiple forms of verified ID in search results.

Using the Airbnb verification process to demonstrate credibility is covered in greater depth on page 288 in the *Building Trust and Getting 5-Star Reviews* chapter.

Ensuring Calendar Accuracy to Avoid Cancellations

Receiving cancellations from hosts reflects poorly on Airbnb's reliability as a platform for booking short-term travel accommodation.

Airbnb want to ensure that if a guest looks at a host's calendar and sees that a place is available, then the place should actually be available for the guest to then book.

As a reminder of how seriously Airbnb take this, when you first setup your account, you were required to commit to keeping an accurate calendar:

Commit to keeping an accurate calendar

Your calendar should always reflect when you can host, since guests can book available days without requesting approval.

Cancelling disrupts guests' plans. If you cancel because your calendar is inaccurate, you'll be charged a penalty fee and the dates won't be available for anyone else to book.

✓ I Understand

Go Back to Availability Settings

Make sure to login frequently and review or update your calendar. Even if you make no changes, simply visiting your calendar will provide Airbnb with an indication that the calendar is being actively monitored and is accurate.

Linking Your Social Media Accounts

Guests naturally trust friends of friends more so than strangers. If you happen to be connected to a guest through mutual Facebook friends, then the prospective guest will be informed of this.

Make sure to connect your Facebook account to your Airbnb account to take advantage of the Airbnb Social Connections feature:

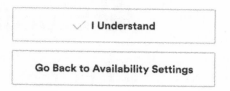

Are you or your friends connected with this host?

f Connect with Facebook

Linking your social media accounts is covered on page 290 in the *Building Trust and Getting 5-Star Reviews* chapter.

Listing on Other Sites

The last couple of decades have seen the emergence and growth of Online Travel Agencies (OTAs). These are websites, like Airbnb, that allow their visitors to book travel-related services, such as short-term rental accommodation.

Airbnb hosts obviously list their properties on *Airbnb*, however some hosts choose to list on other sites like the ones below, in addition to Airbnb too:

 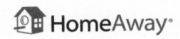

Some of these sites charge a listing fee, whilst Airbnb charge none. These listing fees typically range anywhere between $100 – $1,000.

Instead of charging a listing fee, Airbnb charge a 3% commission "service fee" to hosts, as well as a service fee that ranges between 6-12% of the total booking cost for guests.

For hosts looking for simplicity, they may choose to list exclusively on Airbnb. This gives the added benefit of consolidating good reviews exclusively within Airbnb, which will pay its dividends through greater credibility and additional bookings.

However advertising your listing on multiple sites has the benefit of gaining additional eyeballs reviewing your listing from travelers that are looking for somewhere to stay on other platforms and booking websites too.

Many of these other sites are specifically geared towards hosts that either charge higher nightly rates for their properties, take longer-term bookings, or whom typically list bigger properties that cater to larger-sized parties.

If deciding whether or not to list on multiple sites, hosts should consider what type of property they have and their motivations for hosting, to determine the upside opportunity in listing their place on other sites (and on which other sites that should be too).

Airbnb hosts listing on multiple sites should also ensure that they sync their external calendars with their Airbnb calendar to avoid accidental acceptance of secondary bookings they are unable to accommodate.

Syncing external calendars with your Airbnb calendar is covered on page 176 of the *Booking Settings, Calendar Management and Getting Found* chapter.

Booking Acceptance and Communicating With Guests

Private Messaging on Airbnb

Airbnb have created a dedicated private messaging platform on their site for hosts and guests. All communications prior to bookings need to take place via the platform.

Only registered Airbnb users can use the platform. Becoming a registered user requires providing Airbnb with a valid credit card and uploading a profile photo (as the absolute minimum) for signing up.

Through the platform, all communications can be referenced and followed up. Airbnb also proactively monitor the platform in an attempt to identify fraudulent, malicious or suspicious activity. You can take comfort in knowing that all communications on the system are safe and secure and are taking place on a closed and monitored platform.

In addition to the communication platform that lives on the Airbnb site (and Airbnb mobile app), you'll also receive email notifications from Airbnb too. Any Airbnb communications sent via email will also always be referenceable in message threads that can be found on the Airbnb platform too.

Limitations on the Information You're Able to Share

The messaging platform will attempt to identify and censor certain types of information that hosts and guests try to share prior to a confirmed reservation.

This is principally to prevent lost revenue to Airbnb from bookings that hosts and guests try to arrange outside their platform. It nonetheless also protects you from individuals seeking to carry out sly or malicious behavior through the Airbnb platform. Censored communications include things like personal contact information.

Hosts want to feel comfortable with prospective guests before accepting a reservation request. One downside of this limitation is that it makes it difficult for you to acquire supplementary information when undertaking your "due diligence" on enquiring guests.

Communication Tactics for "Filling in the Blanks"

Despite this limitation, there are still ways and means to learn about your guests on the platform prior to accepting reservation requests.

If you are uncertain about the trustworthiness of a prospective guest, gain additional comfort by seeking further validation of their identity; as well as politely messaging them to understand more about who they are, the purpose of their trip, who will be traveling, as well as anything that helps you get a feel for who they are in their day-to-day lives.

You'll either end up with specific information that'll provide the comfort you're looking for, or give you a gut feeling that something doesn't quite add up.

Be courteous in your requests for information, and explain that you simply like to understand who you're opening up your home to. You're also able to emphasize your desire to better understand your guests so as to provide the best possible hosting experience to them upon their arrival.

Remember to remain compliant with Airbnb's Non-Discrimination Policy when asking any personal or probing questions.

Providing Information Prior to Confirmed Reservations

Do not share personal information prior to having accepted a booking. If a guest wishes to see your place prior to booking, contact Airbnb – they're able to assist you in organizing a viewing. It's also a fairly uncommon request and entirely reasonable to decline if this is something you do not wish to do.

Providing Information After a Confirmed Reservation

Despite having the ability to communicate with your guest via telephone or personal email channels, try keep as much of your communications as is practical on the Airbnb platform for ongoing safety, referencing and protections.

Responding to Booking Inquiries and Reservation Requests

Many hosts will have enabled Instant Book. For these hosts, the need to respond to reservation requests will not be necessary since guests will be able to book these places provided they meet Airbnb's Instant Book requirements.

However, guests who do not meet the requirements must still send a reservation request. And for hosts that have not enabled Instant Book, prospective guests will still need to send a reservation request (even if they would have otherwise satisfied the Instant Book requirements).

It is important to understand the difference between a *booking inquiry* and a *reservation request*. They are similar, yet different in a few crucial ways:

A **booking inquiry** is a non-committal message from a guest to a host to inquire about booking specific dates. In response, the host can send a message, pre-approve, send a Special Offer, or decline the inquiry.

A **reservation request** is a committed request to stay at a place from a guest to a host for specific dates. In response, the host will need to either accept or decline the request within 24 hours before it expires.

Regardless of whether the guest sends a booking inquiry or reservation request, hosts will receive an email notification advising when either of these are received.

You can compare what each of these email notifications looks like on the following page.

Booking Inquiry:

Respond to Michelle's enquiry

Michelle
On Airbnb since 2016

Hi Thomas,

My name is Michelle. I'm coming to NYC on Friday 17th Feb – Mon 20th Feb with my family for a mini getaway. I was wondering if you would give us the pleasure of using your apartment throughout our trip - it looks like a lovely place!

Kind Regards,
Michelle

Pre-approve / Decline

Family-friendly Dream NYC Apartment
Entire home/apt

Friday,
February 17, 2017

Monday,
February 20, 2017

Guests
5

Reservation Request:

Confirm/Deny

Respond to Simon's Request
3 nights at Family-friendly Dream NYC Apartment

Simon
Brisbane, Australia
Airbnb member since 2017

Hello Thomas,

I would like to come stay at your apartment. I am travelling with my wife around the US and would love to spend a weekend in New York.

Your place looks great and is close by to one of our good friends.

I look forward to hearing back from you.

Trip details

Check-in
Fri, Feb 17
Checkout
Mon, Feb 20
11AM

Guests
2

Potential earnings

Based on your rate of $260 per night along with associated fees, your potential payout for this reservation is **$834**.

A key distinction between a reservation request and a booking inquiry is the effect each have on your calendar.

If the **reservation request** is approved, Airbnb will continue to block out the dates as a *confirmed trip*. Other prospective guests will be unable to submit additional reservation requests for overlapping dates until you have approved or declined the initial request. If the request is declined, Airbnb will free up those dates to again enable you to receive new reservation requests from other prospective guests.

On the other hand, a **booking inquiry** will not block the desired dates on your calendar, and will allow you to accept other reservation requests that come through after the booking inquiry has been received.

The following page illustrates an example of a reservation request for *17 – 20 February*. Note the difference in effect that approving or rejecting the reservation has on the calendar for those dates.

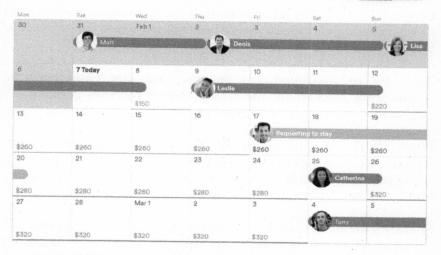

RESERVATION APPROVED   OR   RESERVATION REJECTED

17th – 20th Feb **blocked** with booking

17th – 20th Feb again **available** for other bookings

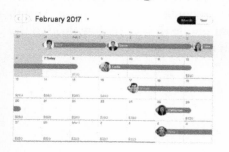

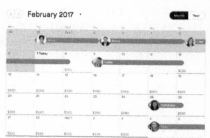

If you receive a reservation request, do not allow it to expire as a means of declining it. Respond to all reservation requests within 24 hours, irrespective of whether you choose to accept or decline it. Failure to do so will impact your response rate, which will also negatively affect your placement in future search results.

Since the dates included on a pending reservation request will be automatically blocked on your calendar, other potential guests won't be able to request them – another reason you'll want to respond ASAP.

If you receive a booking inquiry and *do* wish to host the guest, you may want to create a sense of urgency that prompts the prospective guest to act sooner rather than later in an effort to convert the booking inquiry into a confirmed reservation.

Strategies for doing so include advising the prospective guest that you would suggest booking at their first available convenience in light of peak season demand or other inquiries received for overlapping dates.

Remember that it is entirely up to you whether or not to accept a reservation request. The only thing to bear in mind is that declining a high number of reservation requests will adversely impact your placement in search results.

When you receive a booking inquiry or reservation request, in addition to the email notification, you'll also receive an alert on your Airbnb Dashboard and a notification on your phone (if you've downloaded the Airbnb app and/or set up SMS push notifications).

When it comes to responding to reservation requests, your options are:

1. **Accepting** the reservation for the requested dates

2. **Learning more** about the potential guest by sending them a private message (the "response rate" requirement to respond to reservation requests within 24 hours will be satisfied by simply sending a message to the requesting guest)

3. **Declining** the reservation (with the option of providing an explanation to the guest)

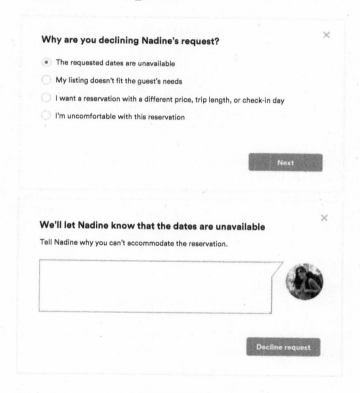

4. Sending the guest a **Special Offer**

Sending Guests a Special Offer

A **Special Offer** allows you to set a custom price for a guest who sends you a booking inquiry or reservation request. Only send a Special Offer if you are ready to confirm a reservation for the inquiring guest.

You can offer multiple guests the same Special Offer for the same (or overlapping) dates. A Special Offer doesn't block dates on your calendar until it is accepted by the guest. Airbnb recommend being open and transparent with your potential guests by letting them know that other guests may be interested in (and potentially book) the same dates too.

If you don't see the option to send a Special Offer, check that the dates on your calendar aren't blocked or that you don't have any pending reservation requests for the same dates. If you do have a pending request from another guest, you'll need to decline it (should you wish) before you can send the Special Offer for any overlapping dates.

If a guest has already submitted a reservation request or has confirmed a reservation, you won't have the option to send a Special Offer for overlapping dates. If you or your guest need to, you can still change the details of an existing reservation by **altering the reservation** (see *Altering an Existing Reservation* on page 238).

To send a guest a Special Offer:
1. Login to Airbnb
2. In **Hosting** mode, select **Messages** from the top navigation bar
3. Open the message thread from the guest you want to send the Special Offer to by clicking on the message thread preview text
4. Click the **Send Special Offer** button

Invite Tony to book by pre-approving this trip

Your calendar is still open until the guest books.

| Pre-approve | Decline | Send Special Offer |

In the **Subtotal** field, enter the price you'd like to offer your guest for their stay. Be sure to include the cleaning fee and/or your additional guest fee in this subtotal, as neither of these are added automatically. If you already have a security deposit on your listing, you don't need to add it to your Special Offer total – it will be included automatically.

Send Tony a Special Offer

Tony will have 24 hours to accept. In the meantime, your calendar will remain open.

Listing

| Family-friendly Dream NYC Apartment | ▼ |

Check In	Check Out	Guests
03-16-2017	03-25-2017	2 ▼

Subtotal

$ 2527

Enter a subtotal that includes any cleaning or extra guest fees. This won't include service fees or applicable taxes.

Your guest will pay $2,744   ∨

You will earn $2,451   ∨

Back   [Send Special Offer]

Once you've sent the guest a Special Offer, Airbnb will notify them. If the guest accepts the Special Offer, the booking will be automatically confirmed.

You have the option of withdrawing the Special Offer at any time prior to the guest accepting it:

Special Offer sent to Tony

Tony has 24 hours to book. You can still accept or pre-approve requests for these dates.

Dates	Guests
Mar 16-25	2

Your guest will pay	You will earn
$2,744	$2,451

Withdraw Special Offer

The guest has 24 hours to respond before the Special Offer expires:

Special Offer expired

Tony didn't respond within 24 hours. You can send them another offer.

Send Special Offer   Pre-approve

The Importance of Remaining Responsive

Your listing's ranking is affected by your responsiveness to reservation requests. Your listing will state your average response time – aim for **within an hour**:

Your Host

Thomas

New York, New York, United States · Joined in April 2013

Response rate: **100%** (past 30 days)

Response time: **within an hour**

Airbnb encourage guests to contact multiple hosts, which means that you are likely not the only host being contacted about a potential guest's booking. Being the first to respond will give you a definitive head-start on winning the booking with all other things being equal.

The easiest way to ensure you're notified of reservation requests immediately as they come though is to download the (free) Airbnb app for your smartphone.

You can also enable push notifications via SMS to your phone. You'll receive an SMS alert every time a new reservation request (and booking inquiry) is received for your place.

Handling Requests for Discounts

Some guests will message you prior to placing a reservation request and ask for a discount. From their perspective, they have little to lose in asking. However, these requests can be frustrating to you as a host. They inevitably require a lot of back-and-forwards communications which take up your time and inevitably raise the administrative overheads in managing your listing.

Furthermore, guests that ask for a discount occasionally indicate a "red flag" for potentially problematic guests. Whilst by no means *always* representing a troublesome guest, these individuals tend to be the type of guests that require a more "hands-on" management style throughout their stay, and will be more likely to cause any number of additional problems that cost you time and money.

Your best strategy is to begin by reflecting on what you *stand to gain* in offering a discount. Some questions to reflect upon are:

- How blocked out is your calendar currently?
- How many days is the reservation request for?
- What day(s) of the week is the reservation request for?
- What impact would accepting this reservation request have on being able to accept other reservation requests?
- What vibe are you getting from the prospective guest in terms of potential concerns throughout the stay?

Once you've determined the desirability of accepting the particular booking to *you*, consider the availability of alternative booking options for the *guest* requesting the discount.

If you live in a big city with lots of Airbnb listings, chances are that if you say *no*, the prospective guest can comfortably accept this fact, and move on with their search to find an alternative listing of comparable price, quality and amenities.

If, on the other hand, the current competition is low, or your place represents something that makes it unique amongst a scarcity of comparable listings, then you are in a much stronger bargaining position to deny the request or offer only a minimal discount.

Smart Negotiation Tactics

Use smart negotiation tactics when getting back to the request for a discount. A few strategies you may wish to consider include...

"Calling their bluff" by suggesting the likelihood that your place will be booked by other full-paying guests. An example response may be:

> *"Thank you for your enquiry. We receive a lot of reservation requests over the summer, so we're unfortunately unable to accommodate requests for discounts throughout these months."*

Communicate additional value that guests will gain by choosing your place over alternatives. Things like unique amenities or higher-quality features encourage prospective guests to see the full charge as an investment in a superior experience rather than an unnecessary expense. An example response may be:

> *"Thank you for your enquiry. Unfortunately our costs cover the additional amenities we provide that separate our place from similar places in the area. We've already discounted our prices despite these value-adds and factored them into our lower prices. We are regrettably unable to provide these superior amenities at rates lower than what they currently are."*

Offer a separate low-cost benefit as an alternative to receiving a discount. Most people simply want to feel like they've walked away a winner, and providing a token benefit transforms the negotiation from a "zero-sum game" of winner/loser into a scenario with a win-win outcome for both you and the guest. You may wish to offer the prospective guest something like a complementary welcome gift upon arrival or free tickets to a local tourist attraction.

Similarly, **provide a discount for future reservations.** Guests will infrequently take you up on this, but still enables you to make them feel like they've walked away a winner despite having no consequence to your current profitability. And in the event that they do take you up on the offer, it will assist your future occupancy rates with an additional booking too.

After the Reservation is Confirmed

After a reservation is confirmed, both parties are given each other's full name and phone number.

You will receive a reservation confirmation email to let you know about the upcoming reservation, which will include a link to view the full itinerary on Airbnb:

You can also get this information by logging into Airbnb and going to **Your Reservations.**

Should you wish, you're able to continue messaging your guest through the Airbnb messaging platform.

Your guest will also receive their itinerary containing useful information about the reservation, such as the **check-in** and **check-out times**, your **address** and **contact information**, as well as access to their **receipt**, your **house rules** and **house manual**:

Whilst non-obligatory, you should also send a welcome email. This will typically include confirmation of the trip details, information on how the guest is able to get to your home from common arrival points (e.g. airports, train stations, etc.), and questions that clarify check-in details (e.g. arrival time, possession of cars and need for parking, etc.). Creating a high-quality template email will enable you to re-use it for each reservation you receive.

The purpose of such an email is twofold:

1. It demonstrates that you're a friendly, communicative and contactable host.
2. It helps you understand where your guests are arriving from and at what time. You can then use this information to provide useful information on how to get to your place to ensure a seamless check-in process (which you'll be rated on shortly).

These days, many guests use the text messaging app *Whatsapp*. Upon confirmation of a reservation, you will receive your guest's mobile phone number. Using Whatsapp is especially useful for communicating with international guests who aren't on your local country's telecommunication network. Alternatively, standard SMS works just as effectively for local guests from your country too.

Once you've downloaded the app to your phone and added your guest's name and phone number to your contacts, you'll be able to see if they too have the app, and if they do, you can send them a text message:

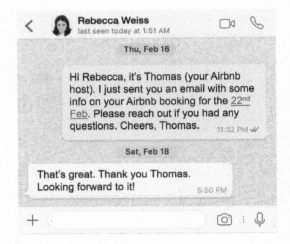

Even if you send your guests an introductory email, it's still a good idea to also send them a brief text message too. You may wish to introduce yourself or let them know that they're able to contact you through that number (or Whatsapp) if they have any questions. You can even let them know that you've also sent them an introductory email too.

Despite the usefulness of alternative communication options like text messaging, calling and private email channels; try default to communicating via Airbnb's private messaging system on the Airbnb platform after having established these other communication channels. Doing so will streamline messages into a single repository both you and your guest are able to reference again in the future, and provide a heightened level of safety and accountability.

You also have an opportunity to develop a House Manual which explains features of your listing (such as how to gain access to the building or apartment). Guests will have access to your house manual once they've confirmed a booking.

To avoid repeating yourself in the introductory email and house manual, you may simply wish to reference the existence of your house manual in the introductory email. However, make sure that key information like how to get to your place is included in the introductory email nonetheless. Many guests will continue to reference your house manual throughout their trip too.

House Manuals are covered in greater detail on page 259 in the *Providing a Phenomenal Guest Experience* chapter.

Communications During a Guest's Stay

Throughout your guest's stay, ensure that you remain both *proactively* and *reactively* communicative.

Proactive Communication

There's no easier way of winning brownie points with guests than proactively checking in with them to ensure that everything is going well.

Nine times out of ten everything will be fine, and they'll appreciate you taking the time to have checked. Occasionally, there'll be a small question at the back of their mind – *where do you keep the extra towels? How do you work the television? Where's the closest train station?*

In both scenarios, taking the time to have checked in on them will not only pre-empt or resolve any issues, but will likely pay its dividends in positive reviews too.

Reactive Communication

Guests may occasionally get in touch to raise an issue or ask you a question. Sometimes these will be fair and understandable, whist other times they may be petty, silly or obvious.

Regardless of your thoughts on the matter, do everything within your power to answer their question, remedy their issue or fulfil their request. Your default position should be a willingness to accommodate the wishes of your guests wherever reasonably practical.

In the eyes of your guest, you are in the *hospitality* business, and within reason, the principle that *the customer is always right* still remains.

Most guests are considerate and reasonable and will not require a disproportionate investment of your time to ensure you are left with a glowing review. Over-investing in the occasional "bad egg" is a small price to pay to guarantee that your good ratings and reviews are maintained.

Take a big picture perspective, and see these "over-investments" as being diluted amongst the vast majority of other trips you host that do not require such hands-on, time-intensive management.

In many instances, guests take issue not with the particular problem they may be having, but rather the lack of its acknowledgement or efforts to have it fixed. Simply acknowledging the guest's issue and demonstrating a desire to get it resolved is normally more than enough to placate an otherwise problematic guest.

Many issues or problems that a guest will raise with you are also likely to be issues or problems that will resurface for future guests too. It is therefore in your interest to fix these for the guest that brings them to your attention with the view that this will benefit future guests and avoid foreseeable problems for you in the future too.

These "annoying" guests will also provide an insight into the type of things that may be specifically important to your target guests, but which have flown under the radar up until then. They therefore represent big opportunities for continually improving your hospitality standards on Airbnb.

You may on occasion be requested or choose to issue a guest with a partial refund in lieu of an issue that a guest brings to your attention.

Use your discretion, but again, if the request is not unreasonable and the amount not too substantial, then consider paying it to make the problem disappear. Regardless of whether you're technically obligated to, this may represent a small price to pay to avoid a bad review or dealing with an official complaint. It will assist in entrenching your long-term Airbnb success.

Altering an Existing Reservation

There may be occasions where you wish to make alterations to a future or current confirmed reservation.

Maybe your guests wish to extend their stay by a day or two. Maybe your guests wish to invite a few more people to join them in your place? Or maybe you need to increase or decrease your prices to reflect changes to these or other circumstances?

Whatever the reason – Airbnb provide the ability to make changes to a confirmed reservation by submitting a reservation alteration request to your guest.

You can do so from a few different places within the Airbnb platform.

One way is to select the relevant reservation directly from your calendar:

1. Login to Airbnb
2. In **Hosting** mode, select **Listings** from the top navigation bar
3. Select **Calendar** for your listing
4. Click on the reservation you wish to alter
5. Click on the **"Alter or Cancel"** link at the bottom of the reservation summary box that will appear on the right

Alternatively, to alter the reservation:

1. Login into Airbnb
2. In **Hosting** mode, scroll down to **Reservations** on your hosting dashboard and select **View all reservations**
3. Find the reservation you need to cancel
4. Select **Change or Cancel** under **Details** for the relevant reservation

4. Select **Change reservation**

Change or cancel Simon's reservation
Feb 17th – Feb 20th at Family-friendly Dream NYC Apartment

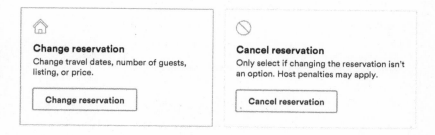

Make the relevant changes to the reservation on the screen that pops up. You'll have the option of changing the **number of guests, check-in** or **check-out date** and reservation **subtotal** (*see next page*).

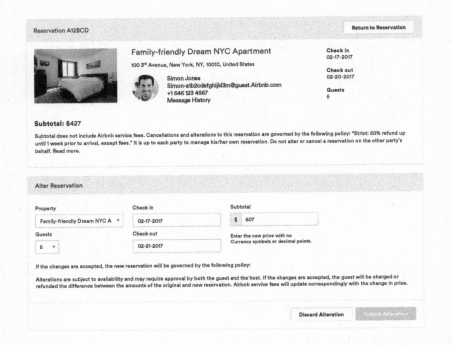

After clicking the Submit Alteration button, you will be prompted to confirm whether you wish to proceed with the proposed changes:

You will then be presented with a summary of the reservation alteration. It will show the original reservation details as well as the proposed altered reservation details:

Family-friendly Dream NYC Apartment

100 3rd Avenue, New York, NY, 10010, United States

Simon Jones
Simon-a1b2cdefghijkl3m@guest.Airbnb.com
+1 646 123 4567
Message History

Original Details

Property	Family-friendly Dream NYC Apartment
Check-In	02-17-2017
Checkout	02-19-2017
Number of guests	5
Subtotal	$427
Service Fee	-$13
Total	$414
Cancellation Policy	Strict: 50% refund up until 1 week prior to arrival, except fees

New Details

Property	Family-friendly Dream NYC Apartment
Check-In	02-17-2017
Checkout	02-20-2017
Number of guests	2
Subtotal	$607
Service Fee	-$18
Total	$607
Cancellation Policy	Strict: 50% refund up until 1 week prior to arrival, except fees

This alteration request is pending. You will be notified when there is a response.

Cancel Request

Your guest will be sent details about your requests to alter the reservation which they will then be able to accept or decline. If the guest accepts your reservation alteration, the reservation details will be updated automatically within Airbnb. If the guest declines your reservation alteration, the reservation details will not change.

You will be informed about their response via email:

Simon accepted your Request

Family-friendly Dream NYC Apartment

We've already updated the reservation and you can see the changes reflected on your itinerary.

View Updated Itinerary

View Your Calendar

Communicating After the Stay

There is no requirement to follow-up with your guest after their stay is complete. Nonetheless, it is exactly for this reason that getting in touch following their trip's conclusion will stand out and be appreciated.

Saying "Thank You"

Thank your guest for staying at your place, and let them know it was a pleasure hosting them. Post-trip thank you notes provide friendly closure on the guest's travel experience. As a non-obligatory gesture, doing so should validate their great stay or smooth out any unpleasantness that took place throughout the booking.

In both scenarios, the guest is more likely to look back favorably on their stay, or be more inclined to overlook anything that was less than favorable. All of this adds up to a higher likelihood of receiving a better guest review.

Request a Review

Guests are also encouraged, but not obliged, to review their hosts upon the completion of their stays. Airbnb will send them a notification reminding them and encouraging them to do so - but the guest is still able to ignore these requests should they so choose.

Writing a personal note at the completion of the stay – especially one that kindly requests the completion of the review process and emphasizing the criticality of reviews as being the lifeblood of hosting on Airbnb – will provide an additional and personalized impetus for the guest to do so.

You're also able to let the guest know that you'll be positively reviewing them, which should hopefully result in a reciprocal positive review from them to you too.

Being strategic with the timing of reviews is covered in greater detail on page 309 in the *Building Trust and Getting 5-Star Reviews* chapter.

Provide Future Discounts

Many hosts offer small discounts (typically 5-10%) for return stays. You're also able to offer your guest a discount that they're able to pass on to friends and family as well.

If they or their friends and family take you up on the offer, you've gained the benefit of having secured an additional reservation and future revenue. If they don't, you've still provided added value and something that can only increase the likelihood of receiving positive reviews after having left a good taste in their mouth.

Example

Below is an example note you may wish to adapt for sending to a guest following the immediate conclusion of their trip:

> *Hi,*
>
> *I just wanted to say thank you for choosing to stay at my place. It was a pleasure hosting you, and you are welcome back anytime in the future! I'll be sure to be writing a positive review.*
>
> *If you too had a good trip, could I please ask that you complete the review process and share any thoughts on your experience. It only takes a couple of minutes, and reviews truly are the lifeblood of hosting on Airbnb. I'd be super appreciative!*
>
> *As a small token of appreciation, I offer a 5% discount on any future stays for previous guests whom I have enjoyed hosting. If you ever return and need somewhere to stay, please send me a message and I'll get back to you with a Special Offer.*
>
> *Thank you once again.*

The Check-In Process

Check-In Times

Hosts have three options for check-in times:

1. Specifying a check-in "window" (anytime between 8am through till 2am the following day)
2. Specifying only one end of the check-in window (e.g. check-in any time after 3pm)
3. 24-hour check-in

If no check-in time is specified, check-in will be set as 3:00 PM local time.

Guests will not see your check-in and check-out times until they visit your listing page from the search results:

The space		
	Accommodates: 5	Check In: Anytime after 3PM
	Bathrooms: 2	Check Out: 11AM
	Bedrooms: 2	Property type: Apartment
	Beds: 3	Room type: Entire home/apt
	House Rules	

These times are unlikely to be the decisive "make-or-break" factor for most guests, however check-in and check-out times that are too restrictive or narrow may prove to be a disincentive for guests that require flexibility in the timing of their arrival and departure (e.g. business travelers).

You should therefore be as open and flexible as possible when determining your check-in (and check-out) times.

Early Check-In's... a Word of Warning

Aside from your personal availability or willingness to meet and greet guests at different times of the day, the time required to clean and turnover your space should be the other key determinant in setting check-in and check-out times. **Ensure that the times you set provide you with enough time to clean and turnover your place between guests.**

You should think twice about providing an early check-in to your home if this means providing guest access before a time that you've had your place cleaned and turned over after the previous guests have left.

All guests will inevitably form first impressions upon arriving anywhere new. Your home is no exception. Your attempts to do an act of goodwill may inadvertently backfire from guests that pre-judge your home on their immediate arrival.

Provide early check-in's only when it has minimal impact to you and does not affect your ability to have your place cleaned and turned over entirely before arrival.

If an early check-in is requested and this is not possible, attempt to provide a practical alternative. For example, suggest going to a local coffee shop (where you may also wish to negotiate a special deal in return for sending them a continual influx of new customers). Opportunities like these can then be shared in pre-trip communications with prospective guests and even promoted as a value-add for your Airbnb listing.

Business Travel Ready and Check-In's

Hosts that wish to have their listings marked as "Business Travel Ready" are required to provide 24-hour check-in. This means that travelers are able to check-in anytime, whether via keyless entry, a lockbox, or by someone who can meet and greet them with the key.

Business Travel Ready listings are covered in greater detail on page 199 in the *Booking Settings, Calendar Management and Getting Found* chapter.

Providing Access to Your Home

Through your pre-trip communications, you will have used the Airbnb messaging system to coordinate check-in and check-out times, explain how to get to your home, overview home amenities and other important information, and answered any other questions your guest may have had.

However, there is no formal online check-in process. Hosts have a number of options for checking-in guests and providing access to their place:

- Being **there in person**
- Having **someone else** come and meet the guests
- Utilizing **key exchange services**
- Installing **keyless door locks**
- Leaving keys in a **lockbox**

Remember that **check-in** is one of the six review criteria you're assessed against. Furthermore, if you get check-in right, you're off with a head-start on everything else. Get check-in wrong and you've left a bad taste in your guests' mouth from the get-go of their trip.

Each of the check-in options is overviewed in greater detail below.

Being There in Person

Pro: Personalization and guest appreciation
Con: Personal time commitment

It is not an Airbnb requirement for you to physically meet your guests in person. Nonetheless, being there to meet and greet your guests face-to-face still remains the "first prize" for guest check-in's.

Some of the benefits include:

- **Adding a "human" element** with the opportunity to share local knowledge, insider tips and recommendations from a *real human* who's there in person
- **Alleviating guest anxieties** around being in a new place and providing guests with the opportunity to gain answers to questions they may otherwise not have asked
- Increasing the likelihood that guests will **respect and take care of your space and property**
- Providing a **more effective and efficient opportunity to explain your space** that saves you from phone calls, text messages and emails further down the track
- Giving you **early indicators of "red flags"** that signal potential problematic guests you're then able to monitor more closely or strategize ways of avoiding problems with
- **Better understanding your target guests** by seeing firsthand who they are, how they found you and what they plan on doing – all useful intel for gaining additional reservations and pleasing future guests

All of this adds up to better reviews and greater profitability.

An important caveat is that you should always attempt to gauge just *how much* or *how little* the guest wishes for you to provide assistance or engage in having a chat.

Your guests may be arriving late at night and might simply want to go to sleep. Your guests may have traveled a great distance and possibly want some personal downtime. Or maybe your guests are just not "people persons" and would prefer to just be left alone.

Whatever the case, use your common sense and social awareness to provide the appropriate interaction. Even if you feel you're able to give them so much more, your willingness to be there in person in and of itself should count for a lot in the eyes of your guests.

The principal challenge when meeting your guests in person is simply the time investment required for doing so. Work and social commitments, travel times and early / late check-in's are all potential impediments to wanting or being able to actually meet your guests in person.

Many hosts also wish to "scale" their Airbnb efforts in a way that drives efficiency and minimizes their personal time commitment. A key element of this is replacing any task that can be automated with a process that doesn't require their personal hands-on involvement.

With alternative options like key exchange services, keyless door locks and leaving keys in a lockbox – you may decide that these alternative options represent a more suitable solution for your situation and desired level of personal commitment. Remember that even if you possess a lockbox or install keyless door locks, you're still able to meet your guests in person upon their arrival - they are not mutually exclusive options.

Many new hosts choose this approach when starting off on Airbnb since the number of guests are traditionally lower and these "hands-on" personal interactions will assist them in learning the ropes and understanding their guests.

Hosts are also more likely to receive positive reviews, and being there in person serves as an appropriate vantage point for deciding whether any of the other options for providing access to their home may or may not be more appropriate.

Having Someone Else Meet Your Guest

Pro: Personalization and guest appreciation
Con: Reliability of helper

For many hosts, meeting their guests in person is simply not practical due to personal schedules, time constraints or other pre-existing commitments. For other hosts, meeting guests in person represents a bigger commitment to Airbnb than they signed up for.

Whatever the reason, hosts wishing to have someone meet their guests in person may still consider having a friend, family member, neighbor or other co-host come meet the guest on their behalf. Almost all of the benefits of personally meeting guests *yourself* remain, but with a few small caveats.

These people are your *ambassadors*. They therefore need to be equally likeable, equally knowledgeable and equally capable of providing the assistance a "live" host is expected to provide for your place. They should also be equally capable of spotting "red flags" and able to relay any concerns or issues back to you.

Having someone else meet and greet your guests will inevitably result in personally forfeiting a lot of the learnings that would otherwise come from the personal interaction of welcoming your guests yourself. These include hearing the questions of incoming guests, learning how guests came to find you and understanding what guests plan on doing throughout their trip.

In the absence of these learnings, your ability to continually improve your understanding of your target guests, how you're able to win more bookings and how you're able to better please your guests will be somewhat constrained.

Depending on your circumstances, having someone else be available to meet your guests might be best kept as an option relied upon for rare occasions or emergencies. Alternatively, you may wish to formalize their involvement by making them an official Airbnb co-host.

Inevitably, asking favors while you profit may cause a misalignment in expectations between yourself and whomever you ask to help out. If having someone else meet your guests becomes the standard means of providing access to your home, you may wish to consider remunerating or providing meaningful gifts to whomever helps you out.

Key Exchange Services

Pro: Host and guest convenience
Con: Limited to hours of shop / office operations

Key exchange services utilize a network of local shops and offices that act as key handover points for your guests. Larger key exchange services have multiple locations around town, which often represents an opportunity to find a key handover spot close to your home.

Hosts pay a monthly fee plus an additional fee for each time a key is picked up. Some of the more sophisticated services allow you to track the location of your keys from a smartphone app. Some also offer 24-hour pickups from select locations in the event of a late arrival (or when the more numerous local key exchange shops or offices are already shut for the day).

Similarly, other services provide a 24/7 "front desk" where guests are able to pick up keys at any time on any day of the week, or will even drop keys off to guests arriving at your property for a fee.

Keyless Door Locks

Pro: Host and guest convenience
Con: Lack of personalization

Keyless door locks are a great option for hosts that are unable to be present at their homes at the time of a guest's arrival.

They eliminate the need for guests to inconvenience themselves with key exchange services, and eliminate your need to re-key locks and replace keys when they get lost. They also assist big groups by allowing everyone within their party to come and go as they please without needing to coordinate the sharing of a limited number of sets of keys.

Keyless door locks enable the guest to gain access to the home using a code which is provided to them prior to their arrival. They provide the ability to issue new codes and replace old codes, thus ensuring that the guest's ability to access your home is limited exclusively to the duration of their stay (much like a security key card at a hotel).

Many digital door locks enable you to create new codes or delete old codes remotely from your computer or smartphone. Some also enable you to receive email or text message notifications and alerts to let you know when codes have been used, who's entered your property and when they've done so.

Digital keyless door locks do not work on all doors however. Where this is the case, small modifications to the door are commonly able to be made to make them compatible.

Hosts that live in apartment buildings may have the unique challenge of having a front door to their building (on the ground floor) that is locked in addition to their personal apartment door. Even if a digital door lock were installed on the host's apartment door, guests may still need keys to gain access to the building first. If this is the case, digital keyless door locks represent a limited remedy in providing guests access to your place.

Below are two popular keyless door locks used by Airbnb hosts:

August Smart Lock

- Safe and secure keyless access to your home with iOS and Android smartphones
- Control who has access to your home and manage how long their access lasts
- Replaces the interior portion of compatible deadbolts in about ten minutes, leaving exterior hardware unchanged

Schlage Keypad Deadbolt

- Create and delete up to 19 access codes
- Installs in minutes with no wiring needed
- Low battery indicator and back-lit keypad

Leaving Keys in a Lockbox

Pro: Host and guest convenience
Con: Lack of personalization

Lockboxes are small key safes that are attached to secure places on your property such as a wall, door, gate or inside an unlocked mailbox.

The lockbox contains physical keys to open your property and is itself only openable with a code.

Similar to keyless door locks, you provide the code to your incoming guests prior to their arrival and they simply enter the code, open the lockbox, get the key and then gain access your home.

It is a convenient solution for hosts that are unable to be physically present to meet and greet their guests, or are unable or unwilling to have someone else open the home on their behalf.

Despite the convenience, this option is not without its risks. Lockboxes represent a safer option than leaving the key under a rug or hidden in a pot plant, but are still not impenetrable by a thief or someone wishing to open it. They also "shine a spotlight" on the fact that within the lockbox are likely to be a set of keys that open the door to a home in the area close by to the lockbox.

Prudent hosts should change the code frequently, otherwise they risk previous guests maintaining continued access to their place. Changing codes frequently may not always be practical for hosts that have a high turnover of guests or do not wish to return back to their property after every stay at their place.

Both the *Master Lock 5400D* (freestanding) and *Master Lock 5401D* (wall-mounted) are two of the more popular lockboxes used by Airbnb hosts:

Keys and Locks

How Many Sets Of Keys?

If you've decided you are going to provide access to your home using traditional lock and keys, then you'll need to provide your guests with a set of those keys.

A common question is *how many sets of keys should be made up?* The answer is **no less than five**. Those five sets should be made for the following people and purposes:

2 sets for your **guests**

2 sets for **yourself**

Your principle set + a spare set you keep for guests in the event that they lose one of their sets

1 set for a **neighbor** or **friend**

They should live close by or be able to help out in the event that you're not available

Fully-Functional Locks

Ensure that your locks work without issue.

It is not uncommon for older homes to have locks that require some jiggling and fiddling or require keys to be inserted in a particular way. These may just be little known quirks to *you*, but are overwhelmingly frustrating or challenging to your *guests*.

It is a reasonable expectation that the keys and locks simply work without complication. Anything less may result in middle-of-the-night phone calls, call-outs to open up for locked-out guests, plus a likely negative review.

Providing a Phenomenal Guest Experience

Providing Little Touches for Big Rewards

Airbnb guests are not looking for cookie-cutter accommodation options. They are discerning travelers frequently wanting one-of-a-kind experiences with personalized touches.

Great Airbnb hosts go the extra mile and provide additional amenities or value for their guests.

These are often small, inexpensive things such as a welcome basket of snacks, chocolates on the pillow, basic toiletries and beauty products, or complementary tickets to the cinema or a local tourist attraction.

These little perks go a long way in impressing guests.

They greatly increase the likelihood of receiving positive reviews and put credit in the "goodwill bank" for when small things go wrong (which inevitably happens on occasion).

Providing these little perks also enhances your listing's desirability by allowing you to mention them on your Airbnb listing and thus provide a differentiating dimension of your place from your competition.

And whilst these perks inevitably cost a small amount to buy, they will almost always pay for themselves many times over through positive reviews, an increase in your number of bookings and a higher price you're able to command for your place as a result.

House Manuals

Your House Manual explains features of your listing, such as how to turn on the hot water heater or where guests can find an extra blanket. Guests receive this information once you've confirmed the reservation – it isn't included on your listing page.

House manual
Give guests tips about your listing, like how to access the internet or turn on the hot water

ACCESS TO HOME:
One key provides access to both the front door of the building, as well as the apartment located on Level 2 within the building. Guests are provided with 2 keys to access the building / apartment. If they have a car, they are also provided with a remote control to open the parking lot gate and roller-shutter garage within the parking lot. Access to the building is also possible via the back door of the ground floor lobby from the carpark using the same key.

ALARM CLOCK:
Each room has two alarm clocks – located on the bedside tables next to each bed. The alarm clock has a high-low dimmer, dual alarm, FM/AM radio, snooze control, sleep and nap functions.

BUZZER AND INTERCOM:
The buzzer / intercom is located next to the front door of the apartment. You will hear a loud buzz sound if a visitor rings from outside. To speak with the visitor, simply lift the telephone off the intercom device and start talking (you do not need to press any buttons whilst talking). To enable visitor access into the building, press the small rectangular black button on the right at the top of the intercom device.

CLEANING SUPPLIES:
Cleaning supplies are stocked under the kitchen sink. You'll find disinfectant spray and liquid, window and mirror spray, carpet stain remover, sponges and scourers, a dustpan and brush. A mop and bucket can be found on the shelves in the laundry room.

To create a House Manual:

1. Login to Airbnb
2. In **Hosting** mode, select **Listings** from the top navigation bar
3. Select **Manage listing** for your listing
4. Click on **Listing details** from the menu at the top
5. Click the **Edit** button for the **Guest resources** section
6. Enter the house manual content you want to share with your guest in the input box under **House manual**
7. Click the **Save** button

Whilst far from being an exhaustive list, your House Manual should include information on the following things...

 Access: Explain how to access your home; including anything relating to keys, entry codes, gates and locks that guests need to know about.

 Buzzer and intercom: Explain how to operate the intercom and let people into the building.

 Electricity: Explain where the electrical box is located and how to reset electricity in the event of a power shortage.

 Food, drink and coffee: Tell guests about any foods you provide like breakfast, condiments and spices, coffee and tea or anything else they're able to help themselves to. Explain how to operate any coffee machines too.

 Garbage and recycling: Explain the location of garbage chutes and bins. Provide information on garbage pickup days and any relevant recycling information. Let guests know where you store extra garbage bags.

 Gym: Provide instructions for accessing the gym, hours of operation and anything else guests need to know for making use of gym facilities.

Heating and air-conditioning: Explain how to operate and control any heating or air-conditioning units and thermostats within the home.

 Internet and Wi-Fi: Provide your network name, Wi-Fi code and instructions on how to reset the router in the event that the internet stops working.

 Kitchen: Explain how to operate any major appliances such as ovens and stoves.

 Laundry: Explain how to operate washing machines and dryers as well as instructions on where to find any laundry products that you provide, such as detergent.

 Location of home amenities: Explain where guests are able to find additional amenities they may require throughout their stay such as extra blankets or towels.

 Parking: Explain where to park cars and instructions on how to access the garage.

 Pool and hot tub: Provide instructions for accessing the pool and hot tub, hours of operation and anything else guests need to know for making use of pool and hot tub facilities.

 Shower: If you have a complicated shower, explain how to operate it.

 TV and media: Explain how to operate your television, use any remotes and access cable channels, streaming media services (e.g. Netflix, Hulu, etc.) or home media devices (e.g. DVD players).

Guidebooks

The incredible hole-in-the-wall sandwich shop tucked hidden away in that narrow lane may be your local go-to lunch spot, but remains unknown to all but locals.

Many guests will not be from your city, and almost none will be from your local neighborhood. Guests will rarely know the local "go-to" spots that you know like the back of your hand. After all – it's *your* local area and these are the places *you* likely frequent all the time.

Good Airbnb hosts adopt the role of the concierge at the front desk of a hotel – able to assist guests by providing answers to their most frequently asked questions. And the good news is that more times than not, these questions are very commonly the same...

What are the sightseeing attractions I should check out?

Where can I get a good bite to eat? Any stand-out dishes on the menu?

I'm craving a good cappuccino. Does that exist anywhere around here?

I need to keep the kids happy. Any ideas?

I just got sick and need some cold and flu medicine. Is there a 24-hour pharmacy?

Guests often choose to stay with Airbnb hosts largely for their ability to provide these insider tips and use their host's local knowledge to answer questions like the ones above.

Airbnb provide hosts with the ability to proactively answer these questions by creating local guidebooks they're able to make available for their guests. These guidebooks showcase the best that their neighborhood has to offer and helps their listing stand out from the crowd.

⌢ Bars

Flatiron Lounge
37 West 19ᵗʰ Street New York, NY 10011-4200

A solid cocktail spot. Wonderful loungey feel, without being too gimmicky.

Middle Branch
154 East 33rd Street New York, NY 10016

It's hard to come across a proper whiskey cocktail these days. This is your spot!

Albion Bar
575 2nd Ave NY, NY 10016

30 craft beers on tap and a $5 Happy Hour every day until 8pm.

Your guidebook is publicly displayed on your Airbnb listing page (even before guests book your place).

You're also able to print your guidebooks and make them available to your guests in hard-copy format for their arrival at your place.

Airbnb guidebooks represent one of the easiest ways of impressing guests and providing them with a great experience when staying at your place.

Guidebooks enable you to show-off your knowledge of the local area, reinforce your credibility as an Airbnb host "in-the-know", increase the likelihood of receiving reservation requests, as well as maximize the prices you're able to command from guests looking to stay in great spots with reliable hosts.

The key to building a virtuous cycle of increased bookings is through receiving positive reviews. And there's no quicker shortcut to receiving positive reviews than by providing your guests with a guidebook of your local area since **communication, location** and **value** represent 50% of the review criteria that hosts are assessed against: Guidebooks demonstrate a communicative host, living in a great location, providing valued guest experiences.

Finally, the beauty of the Airbnb guidebook is that you'll get your mileage from this small investment by reusing it with all future guests, despite only needing to build it once. As a low-cost, time-minimal investment, building an Airbnb Guidebook truly represents the "low-hanging-fruit" of your Airbnb success.

Places you're able to include in an Airbnb guidebook fall into the following categories:

Food Scene:

Places to grab a bite to eat. This includes your favorite restaurants, cafes and coffee shops, bakeries, desert shops and street markets

Drinks and Nightlife:

Hotspots you like to hang out at night. This includes nightclubs, bars, music venues, breweries, wineries, karaoke and casinos

Sightseeing:

Some of the must-see iconic sights in your city. This includes places of interest, special neighborhoods or famous streets

Parks and Nature:

Places to go to be around nature. This includes places like local, state and national parks, hiking trails and beaches

Arts and Culture:

 Destinations for getting a feel for the local history and culture. This includes places like museums, the theatre, symphony halls, art galleries, schools, universities and libraries

Shopping:

 Any unique or local shops around you. This includes shopping malls, clothing stores, bookstores, markets or any other shops of appeal or interest

Essentials:

 Places to go for everyday errands or basic needs. This includes places of public service, convenience stores, grocery stores, doctors or hospitals, gyms and fitness centers, dry cleaners and laundromats, as well as beauty salons and spa places

Entertainment and Activities:

 Spots to go for having fun. This includes places like movie theatres, amusement parks, aquariums and zoos, arcades and game parlours, tours, classes, sport stadiums or any other sport and recreation in the area

Getting Around:

 Ways and means of traveling around your city. This includes places like public transportation hubs, car rental and repair spots, places to rent bikes and parking lots

Key Principles for Developing Your Guidebook

Build for your target guests: Think about *who* your target guests are. An elderly retired couple will have different interests to a gap-year backpacker. Make sure you include places most likely to be of interest, relevance and within budget of your target guest.

Cover a dispersed regional spread: Guidebooks should offer recommendations for places to be found in your local neighborhood, the city and its surroundings, and everything in-between. Recommend the local coffee shop located at the bottom of your apartment building, but also suggest checking out the art gallery on the outskirts of the city too.

Cater to seasonal variance: Some listings are located in cities that are highly susceptible to seasonal tourism and able to provide a range of seasonal attractions. Useful guidebooks include attractions that cover all seasonal interest, and showcase the best of your location at all times of the year.

How to Add a Guidebook to Your Listing

To create your Guidebook:

1. Login to Airbnb
2. In **Hosting** mode, select **Listings** from the top navigation bar
3. Select **Manage listing** for your listing
4. Click on **Listing details** from the menu at the top
5. Click the **Edit** button for the **Guidebook** section

Once here, hosts can add to their guidebook by typing the name of the place they wish to include within the relevant guidebook category. Airbnb will automatically retrieve the official name of the place you wish to add, which you then select.

 **Food Scene**

What are your favourite restaurants, bakeries, and coffee shops?

Airbnb will also use *Google Maps* to automatically pull the address and a map of the spot you want to list:

You then select a sub-category for the place:

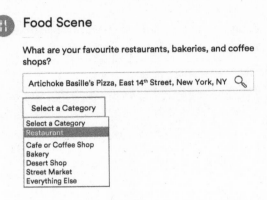

It's then up to you to provide a short description of up to 200 characters for the place you want to list. Use this space to let guests know why you recommend it, why it might be of interest to them, or an "insider tip" they'll appreciate for when they go there. You also have the option of specifying things the place is good for:

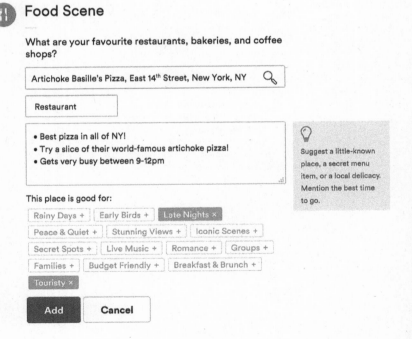

Recommended Places to Include

 Food Scene

Fast Food Restaurants: Sometimes a guest just wants something to eat that's quick, simple and without any surprises. It won't be their best meal, but it also won't be their worst. It'll come cheap and everyone knows what to expect. Fast food restaurants often help guests feel comfortable in new surroundings by providing them with something they're already familiar with from back home.

Local Favorite Restaurants: These are your favorite go-to places to get served up with a local dish or some personal comfort food. They're the kind of place frequented by locals "in-the-know" about where to grab a good bite to eat. You're also likely to be familiar with the best dishes on the menu. Make sure to share these insider tips!

Iconic Restaurants: These are restaurants that have developed a cult following over the years. They have woven themselves into the fabric of the local area, and often reflect the flavor of the neighborhood or community too.

Brand Name Coffee Shops: Just like fast food restaurants, sometimes what guests are really looking for is simply something they're already familiar with from back home. Make sure to include a brand-name coffee spot if one exists close by to your place.

Your Local Favorite Coffee Shop: For true coffee addicts, they need their coffee, and they need it NOW! They'll want to know the best place to get their coffee fix that's no more than a couple of minutes' walk from your place.

Coffee Spots Near Public Transport: Guests are frequently on-the-go and tend to get around by public transport. Many guests will package-up their morning coffee routine with setting off on their daily adventures. It makes sense to include coffee spot recommendations close to public transport hubs like train stations or bus terminals.

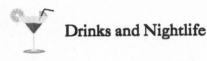 **Drinks and Nightlife**

The Bar-With-a-View: There's nothing more awesome than visiting a bar that overlooks the skyline of the city you're visiting. Rooftop bars with a view are great for this. Obviously, not every city has one, but try recommend a bar that commands the attention of the city you live in.

The Local Bar: Think of these places as your local 'Cheers Bar'... *where everybody knows your name.* Drinks are commonly cheaper, staff friendlier, and no dress shirts or leather shoes required for entry.

The Swanky "It" Bar: These are commonly bars that have only recently opened and have greatest appeal to younger guests wanting to be "in-the-know". Hosts have an opportunity to show-off their knowledge of the local area by offering insider tips unlikely to be found in guidebooks printed any less recently than within the year.

 Parks and Nature

Parks: Entertainment for the kids *and* the parents doesn't need to be an "either/or" decision. Parks provide an excellent balance for parents looking for some personal down-time within a safe and relaxed environment for their kids to enjoy themselves too. Best of all, both parties get some fresh air and hands-on exposure to the local area.

Playgrounds: Turns out, the best things in life *are* sometimes free. Nothing epitomizes this more so than watching a kid enjoy their time at a playground. Local councils often invest small fortunes in building playground structures that represent "kiddie-heaven". Playgrounds are also a great way for parents to get out of the house, entertain the kids, and do so entirely for free. List any playgrounds close by to your place – especially if you attract lots of families with your listing.

Natural Beauty Spots: These include places like popular beaches, hiking trails or national parks. They are often drawcards for visiting the city and the kind of places guests love boasting about having visited to friends and family.

Arts and Culture

Art Galleries and Museums: Some cities have world-renowned art that people travel the globe to see. Other cities have funky little museums that curate the world's largest collection of baseball cards. Either way, guests are likely to be curious on the ways they're able to get their cultural fix with a visit to your city.

Famous Schools, Universities and Libraries: Live near an ivy-league university, or close to a school attended by a famous celebrity? Maybe there's an impressive sandstone library building in relative proximity to your place built many centuries ago? Guests will appreciate the opportunity to simply take a walk past these institutions to feel like they've added a small boost of prestige to their trips.

 Sightseeing

Historical Places: These are places that have become tourist attractions for having been around for many decades, if not centuries. Religious sites, ancient ruins, castles and the like are common examples. They are commonly listed in travel guidebooks, and appeal to travelers or history buffs that often spend a lifetime traveling the globe to cross off their bucket-list.

Novelty Attractions: These are one-of-a-kind places that are unique landmarks unlikely to be found anywhere else. They are often quirky, different or the kind of thing that doesn't fit neatly into any travel guidebook category. They make for interesting stories, and typically even better pictures.

 **Essentials**

Convenience Stores: Sometimes a guest just needs a few basic items like bread, milk and cereal. They'll probably be picking these up on their way home from daily adventures, and appreciate not needing to carry these items for anything more than a few blocks. Letting guests know about the local convenience store, 24-hour gas station or local "corner store" will prove to be a huge help.

Delicatessens: Typically serving up fine foods or gourmet produce, these establishments allow guests to purchase things like cured meats, sausages, pickled vegetables, dips, breads and olives. Many of these "luxury" items will not be available in standard supermarkets or convenience stores, so mentioning these places will help elevate the stature of your listing.

Grocery Stores: Guests that are staying for an extended duration will likely want to stock up on groceries that will carry them through for the duration of their stay. Point them in the direction of the closest place they're able to do a big shop at good prices for all the things they're likely going to want and need.

Pharmacies: The last thing you want to do when feeling under the weather and away from home is trekking out in search of a local pharmacy. Telling guests that they're able to pick up that cold-and-flu medicine by walking no further than the end of the block will win you a lot of brownie points should they run into the dreaded sniffles during a stay at your place.

Phone and Electronics Repair Stores: You'd be amazed at how often phones and laptops die while guests are travelling and away from their homes. The only thing more frustrating than having a broken iPhone is not having the ability to do anything about it. Guests will be thankful to learn there's a local repair shop able to fix their laptop, iPad or phone so they're able to continue posting those holiday snaps on Instagram or Skyping with family back home.

Shopping

Shopping Malls: These represent handy one-stop-shops for guests looking to "batch process" their shopping experience and eliminate the need to jump all over town to find what they're looking for. Everything from department stores through to local and global brands can typically be found here.

Notable Stores: Sometimes there's a store in the neighborhood that's been around since before the neighborhood was even a neighborhood. Whether an old bookstore with local charm, or the antique store still run by its original owner; a casual visit may become an experience no less enjoyable than hopping into a time machine and exploring a bygone era. Other times, a popular TV show or movie may have put a particular store close by on the map. Be sure to let your guests know of any stores they'll likely want to check out or take a picture in front of.

 Entertainment and Activities

Movie Theaters: As a popular and reliable form of entertainment, listing your local cinema will ensure that guests have a near fail-proof option of something to do if and when they're looking to get out of the house. Movies appeal to guests of all types and ages, making them a *must* for any guidebook looking to provide attractions of broad appeal.

Bowling Alleys: Maybe not something guests want to do every day, but knowing where the local bowling alley is can be a great piece of information for parents to keep up their sleeves for entertaining the kids on a rainy day. Mentioning the local bowling alley is a reliable, kid-friendly attraction guaranteed to eliminate a parent's headache when forced to find ways to keep the kids happy and entertained.

Comedy Clubs: Always a crowd-pleaser for guests looking for something to do, comedy clubs typically provide a fun night out at a reasonable price. They tend to be a form of entertainment that guests don't typically do in their own home cities, but are excited to do when visiting somewhere else.

Providing a Guestbook at Your Place

Guestbooks are physical books you keep in your place that allow guests to record their presence in your home and share any thoughts they had on the experience.

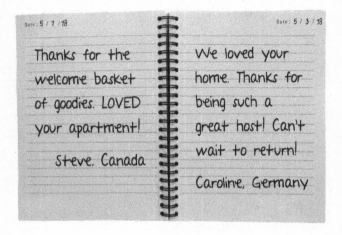

Whilst they are not a requirement of Airbnb, guestbooks serve the benefit of encouraging guests to document their favorite things that they enjoyed about staying at your place.

They will inspire guests to reflect on the positive elements of their trip, which will increase the likelihood of giving positive reviews when asked to review their trip 24-hours after checking out.

They also provide a great source of validation for incoming guests who have the opportunity to flick through a thorough record of other satisfied guests who have enjoyed staying at your place. When left out on display in a public space, they will prime new guests to expect the best and anticipate a positive travel experience of their own.

Guestbooks will also give you insights into the things that guests enjoyed most about staying at your place. You can then use these insights to continually improve your hospitality and focus on providing more of the things you know guests love and appreciate.

Check-Out, Cleaning and Turnover

The Check-Out Process

Despite being of lesser importance from the guest's point of view, check-out remains a critical step in the hosting process for hosts.

Check-Out Time

Set a check-out time that provides maximum flexibility and convenience to your guest but with minimal impact or inconvenience to you. This means knowing...

- How long it takes to clean and turnover your place
- The notice time required to schedule a cleaning
- The check-in and advance notice requirements (e.g. same day, at least one day's notice, etc.) for bookings of future guests

If no check-out time was specified on your Airbnb listing, check-out is **12:00 PM local time.**

You also have the ability to set a **preparation time** between guest stays. Your options include blocking either...

... before and after each reservation

To add a preparation time requirement to your calendar:

1. Login to Airbnb
2. In **Hosting** mode, select **Listings** from the top navigation bar
3. Select **Manage listing** for your listing
4. Click on **Availability** from the menu at the top
5. Click the **Edit** button for the **Reservation preferences** section
6. Select either **Block 1 night before and after each reservation** or **Block 2 nights before and after each reservation** from the drop-down options under **Preparation time**
7. Click the **Save** button

Reservation preferences

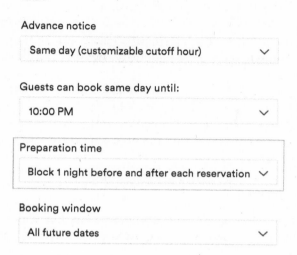

Being There in Person and Checking for Damage

Just like with check-in, being there in person at check-out is always advisable whenever practical.

Being there in person re-activates the "human element" of the hosting process and allows you to confirm that your guests have had a positive experience or address anything that may have been an issue throughout their stay. Both of these outcomes will be important in ensuring you receive the best possible reviews very shortly.

On a practical note, it also allows you to check for damage to your property and possessions.

If you need to make a claim under the Airbnb Host Guarantee or your security deposit, you only have 14 days from your guest's check-out date or before the next guest checks in to do so – whichever is earlier. Many hosts have booked out calendars with back-to-back bookings. Being physically present at check-out may represent one of the few (if not only) opportunities a host has to check for damage before the next booking comes through the door (which may be as early as that same day).

If you will be present at check-out, let your guests know this upon their arrival during check-in. A guest that knows you will be present at check-out is more likely to avoid causing damage to your property knowing that you will personally be there to inspect the place upon their exit. They will also be in a weaker position to deny any wrongdoing for damage that you identify they have caused.

As the final part of their stay at your place, it's also your last opportunity to positively influence their impressions. Remember that within 24 hours of check-out, the guest will be prompted to review and rate their experience. Ensure that you use this final opportunity to leave the best possible taste in their mouth.

What to do with Keys

If you can't be there in person, it's important that you arrange with your guests how they're able to return keys or leave the place locked and secured.

For homes that utilize traditional locks and keys, a common solution is to ask guests to deadlock all doors, place the keys by the door on the inside and then simply close the door behind them on exit. You're then able to return to your place with *your* set of keys, and collect the keys that were left by the guest.

Alternatively, if you use a lockbox, you may ask guests to place the keys back in the lockbox where they were originally taken from. Similarly, you're able to ask guests to return keys to neighbors, key exchange shopfronts or cafes close by – where they may have picked up the keys initially upon arrival.

Cleaning Fees and How Much to Charge

Providing a clean and tidy space will make your guests feel comfortable in your home from the moment they arrive. A clean place demonstrates your commitment to providing a high standard of hospitality and will make your guests feel welcome and at ease.

Some hosts choose to cover the cost of a professional cleaner by including a **cleaning fee**:

Extra charges

Cleaning fee
This fee will apply to every reservation.

$ 100

Security deposit
If you submit a damage claim within 14 days of checkout, guests will be responsible for damages up to this amount.

$

Extra guests
After more than: 1 guest, charge $0 per person, per night.

$

For each guest after

1 ⌄

Weekend pricing
This nightly price will replace your base price for every Friday and Saturday.

$

Cleaning fees help hosts account for any extra expense they incur in getting their place clean and tidy for incoming guests.

The fee is charged once per trip – not as a nightly fee. For example, if a listing has a cleaning fee of $100, the guest does not pay $100 per night – they pay $100 only once, regardless of how many nights the reservation is for.

Consider carefully how much you charge because a big fee can make a one or two night stay very expensive. Getting your cleaning fee *right* means not losing money by charging less than it costs to have your place cleaned and turned over. Getting your cleaning fee *wrong* risks losing potential reservation requests because your prices are perceived as too high.

Because the cleaning fee is included in the total guest payment and host payout, Airbnb's service fees apply on this too. For hosts, this is 3%.

To add a cleaning fee to your listing:
1. Login to Airbnb
2. In **Hosting** mode, select **Listings** from the top navigation bar
3. Select **Manage listing** for your listing
4. Click on **Pricing** from the menu at the top
5. Click the **Edit** button for the **Extra charges** section
6. Enter your cleaning fee into the **Cleaning fee** input box
7. Click the **Save** button

Cleaning fees are not automatically included when making a Special Offer, which should be an all-inclusive price. Keep this in mind if offering a prospective guest a Special Offer for your place.

The Guest's Perspective

In search results, guests see a *total* price inclusive of the cleaning fee (+ Airbnb service fee), to get a better idea of the total cost for the stay.

Below is a sample listing from a search for a place in New York for one night. It quotes a nightly price of $238.

$238 total ⚡ 🏆   ★★★★★ 61 reviews

Central Park Getaway
Entire home/apt · 1 bed · 4 guests · Business Travel Ready

When a prospective guest clicks on the listing from the search results page, they're taken to the specific listing's Airbnb page. Here's the information they see at the top of the listing's page:

Whilst the nightly rate is only $133, adding the cleaning and service fees brings the total to *$238*. Each of these are listed as separate line items in the price breakdown. The key takeaway here is that you **should not over-charge with your cleaning fees**. Doing so may potentially scare off potential guests that would otherwise be interested in your place at a reasonable price.

These potential guests may never even make it to your listing page if they were put off by perceived over-pricing when your place was displayed in search results. Remember that it's not until they arrive at your listing page that they know how much of the total cost relates exclusively to your cleaning fee (vs. the nightly charge for the place itself).

If we compare the total cost for a 1-night vs. 2-night vs. 3-night reservation, we can see that the cleaning fee represents a larger share of the total cost for shorter stays:

NIGHTS	CALCULATION	CLEANING FEE AS % OF TOTAL COSTS
1 night	$133 per night + $79 Cleaning fee + $26 Service fee	33%
2 nights	($133 per night x 2) + $79 Cleaning fee + $42 Service fee	20%
3 nights	($133 per night x 3) + $79 Cleaning fee + $56 Service fee	15%

Whilst the length of a guest's stay is outside of your control, the cleaning fee is not – it is determined entirely by you.

Therefore be aware of the dangers of inflating your cleaning fee as a means of making a quick buck. Whilst you may get away with charging more than the cleaning actually ends up costing you, the additional income you'll receive needs to be weighed up against the risk of losing prospective guests that perceive your place as too expensive and never end up booking.

Additionally, guest perceptions that they're being taken for a ride through an exploitation of the cleaning fee may be enough to scare them off consideration of your place when deciding where they want to book.

In addition to keeping things honest, rarely will a small inflated cleaning fee justify the lost income of additional bookings that would otherwise have come through, but never eventuate.

How Much to Charge

So how much should you actually charge? It's important to remember that whether you pay for a cleaner or do the cleaning yourself, there is a cost (either financial or your personal time) associated with each.

Cleaning fees have become a common feature across most listings on Airbnb. Hosts that do not add a cleaning fee typically compensate with a higher nightly price. Therefore so long as you keep your cleaning fee honest and reasonable, the mere fact of simply having a cleaning fee should have minimal impact on the likelihood of getting booked.

Try keep the cleaning fee as close as possible to the actual cost of getting your place cleaned.

If you're doing the cleaning yourself, another method for determining your cleaning fee is to do a search on Airbnb for comparable listings (same home type, room and bathroom numbers) in your same neighborhood / city, and seeing how much *they're* charging for *their* cleaning fee. Try not to venture too far north of whatever these cleaning fees are. You will want to make sure however that the reasonable value of your personal time factors into the final cost you arrive at.

An emerging service that's becoming increasingly popular for Airbnb hosts are cleaning companies that provide their services specifically for short-term rental properties such as those listed on Airbnb.

As an "on-demand" service you're able to call upon only at the times you have bookings and need your place cleaned, they are a useful and handy service to keep up your sleeve. The downside however is the lack of familiarity with your cleaning and turnover preferences that inevitably results from ad-hoc visits by different cleaners each time.

What Needs to be Cleaned With Each Turnover?

Depending on your place and the extent you wish to provide a premium experience and level of hospitality, you may want to consider doing any or all of the following:

All Rooms

- Clean floor surfaces
- Disinfect, spray and dust surfaces and surface tops
- Empty garbage, recycling and wastebaskets
- Vacuum carpets and rugs
- Wipe down mirrors, windows and glass fixtures (removing all streaks)

Kitchen and Dining Room

- Clean insides and exteriors of fridges, microwaves, ovens and stoves
- Empty and clean the sink
- Remove old food from fridge and pantry
- Wash and put away dirty dishes
- Wipe down tables and arrange chairs

Bathrooms

- Clean and organize vanity units
- Replenish hygiene and beauty products
- Scrub wall tiles
- Wash and sanitize bathtubs, showers, sinks and toilets

Bedrooms

- Make beds with fresh linen
- Tidy closets and make space
- Check for and remove any personal items left by previous guests from drawers and storage units

One Little Trick...

When it comes to keeping your place clean, one little trick is to provide your guests with the ability to tidy up after themselves.

Be sure to leave cleaning supplies so they can take care of spills and accidental messes. You'd be surprised at how often guests take it upon themselves to leave their host's place in a better condition than their very own homes!

Building Trust and Getting 5-Star Reviews

Using the Airbnb Verification Process to Demonstrate Credibility

Airbnb created the **Verified ID process** to build trust in the Airbnb community. It gives hosts and guests more information when deciding who they want to host or stay with on Airbnb.

Airbnb users have the opportunity of verifying their identity by connecting their Airbnb profiles to other social networks as well as scanning official ID and confirming personal details.

What does the ID verification process involve?

- Taking a photo or uploading an image of your government-issued ID (such as your driver's licence or passport)
- Connecting another social media profile to your Airbnb account (such as a Facebook, Google, or LinkedIn account)
- Uploading an Airbnb profile photo and providing a phone number and email address

When you've completed the Verified ID process, you'll earn the Verified ID badge on your profile:

 Verified

Many guests look for this badge when deciding whether they wish to stay with a particular host.

Once you complete the ID verification process, your profile will display all the ways that Airbnb have been able to verify you and your identity.

If we take a look at the example below, we can see that Airbnb have been able to confirm the following things about this particular host:

- They've provided Airbnb with verified forms of government ID such as a driver's licence or passport
- There's personal information you're able to read up about them (e.g. school attended, work and languages spoken)
- They have a real email address
- Airbnb know their phone number
- They have a verified Facebook, Google and LinkedIn account

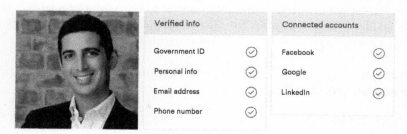

Now imagine you're a guest looking for a place to stay. You're debating between one of two places and could go either way. Both look like good options, but the verified IDs for the hosts of the two places looks like this...

Host 1

Verified info		Connected accounts	
Government ID	✓	Facebook	✓
Personal info	✓	Google	✓
Email address	✓	LinkedIn	✓
Phone number	✓		

VS.

Host 2

Verified info	
Email address	✓
Phone number	✓

Who would you stay with?

Whilst the second host will in most likelihood turn out to be *just* as reliable, *just* as trustworthy and provide *just* as good a hosting experience; most guests will be operating with the mindset *why take a chance?*

Your job is to nip in the bud as many potential concerns that prevent you and your place from being perceived as the natural and obvious choice of where a guest wishes to stay. And there's no easier way of doing that than by verifying your ID and eliminating any trust and safety concerns.

Just as you take comfort in seeing the verified ID badge when screening guests that want to stay at *your* place, so too will guests screen *you* when deciding where *they* want to stay.

The added benefit is that once verified, it is forevermore a badge you can display on your profile for all future prospective guests to see – there's no need to re-verify or renew existing verifications.

You can begin the Airbnb verification process by visiting **www.airbnb.com/verify**.

To add additional verifications:
1. Login to Airbnb
2. Click on your account profile photo in the top right corner
3. Select **Profile**
4. Select **Verify more info** (at bottom of the Verified info box)
5. Select **Connect** for each of the social media platforms (Facebook, Google and LinkedIn) you wish to connect to your Airbnb account

---

Add More Verifications

Facebook

Sign in with Facebook and discover your trusted connections to hosts and guests all over the world.

[Connect]

Google

Connect your Airbnb account to your Google account for simplicity and ease.

[Connect]

LinkedIn

Create a link to your professional life by connecting your Airbnb and LinkedIn accounts.

[Connect]

References

Reviews on Airbnb are only possible from guests that have actually stayed at your place and experienced your hosting style and hospitality first-hand. If you're a new host, you're therefore disadvantaged by the limited time you've been active on Airbnb and the number of times you've been able to host guests.

As a mechanism to help newer (and also long-term) hosts let their good character and hosting potential become known to prospective guests, Airbnb added the ability for hosts to display *references* on their profiles too. Hosts (and guests) can receive public references from friends, family members and colleagues to help build credibility and trustworthiness into their Airbnb profiles.

These references help guests in the Airbnb community get to know you and feel more comfortable before booking to stay with you.

Here is an example of a reference on Airbnb:

Thomas

I had the pleasure of living with Jonathan in his apartment throughout 2017. He proved himself to be a great roommate in addition to being a general all-round great guy! Jonathan was always friendly and caring, as well as considerate to the fact that he shared his apartment with others. I was always made to feel comfortable staying in the apartment with Jonathan. Whilst these are qualities that I got to experience first-hand, I also saw him exhibit these same behaviors with other people too - both within and outside the apartment. It is no surprise that he has the ability to connect with all types of travelers – be they young, old, adventurous or shy. This extends also to the way in which Jonathan maintained the apartment, always ensuring that everyone felt at ease living in a clean and comfortable space. This proved to be especially important in NYC where personal space is often perceived as a luxury and frequently hard to come by. For anyone wanting to deal with a friendly, considerate and down-to-earth person throughout their travels, whilst staying in a well-maintained home – I would have no hesitation in recommending Jonathan!

You're able to request references from people within your personal network. These references will appear publicly on your Airbnb profile to help other members get to know you.

One benefit of references (and difference from reviews) is the ability to review a reference written about you and either accept or decline it before they it is displayed on your public profile.

To request a reference, you have the option of either requesting a personal reference through Facebook messaging or directly from friends already on Airbnb.

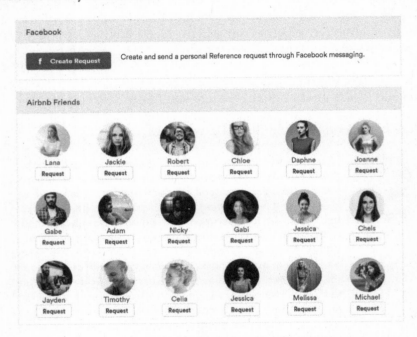

To request a reference, visit **www.airbnb.com/users/references**.

The Importance of Good Reviews

Think about any time you've ever screened applicants for a job that you were hiring for? Or inquired about someone prior to going on a date? Have you ever Googled someone to see what information comes up? Or if nothing else, read a restaurant review before deciding where you were going to have dinner that night?

Reviews, opinions and the perspectives of others matter. They have become key influences that shape our personal decisions across all facets of modern-day life. And Airbnb is no different.

Gaining comfort from the reviews of previous guests is a critical dependency to winning guests that hit the *Book Now* button.

A host's reviews and Airbnb reputation remain the principal driver of building this trust and credibility. As Airbnb explain...

> *Reviews are your opportunity to build a good reputation in the Airbnb community, as well as share your experience with the Airbnb community. Since you can only write a review after a reservation is confirmed on the site, you can trust that any review you see on a profile page is the result of an actual person booking with or hosting another member of the community.*

Would you feel reassured seeing the following if you were a guest looking for a place to stay...

143 Reviews   ★★★★★

Accuracy	★★★★★	Location	★★★★★
Communication	★★★★★	Check In	★★★★★
Cleanliness	★★★★★	Value	★★★★★

Prospective guests will interpret all information you share on your listing through the lens of your prior reviews. Having good reviews will validate the trustworthiness of the representations you make. Having bad reviews will negate those representations, whether truthful or not.

There are a number of important reasons you need to have good reviews on Airbnb, all of which feed off one another to create a virtuous cycle:

Get Found More Often
Hosts with favorable reviews from satisfied guests are prioritized higher in search results by Airbnb, resulting in being found more often

Make More Money
Greater interest and demand means greater ability to command higher prices from more satisfied guests, thus maximizing your earning potential

More Booking Requests
You and your listing will appear more credible, reliable and trustworthy to prospective guests deciding where they want to stay

As such, good reviews become a critical dependency to success on Airbnb. Taking the time to acquire positive reviews is an investment that will pay for itself many times over.

There's a small game of "catch-up" to play for new hosts who don't have the luxury of a long hosting track-record on Airbnb. Especially if starting off as a new host, the most important thing you can do for your ongoing success is expediting the process of getting good reviews.

As a new host, consider strategically discounting your place to maximize bookings (and therefore reviews) as quickly as possible. The value of good reviews will far surpass the "lost" revenue you incur in the short-term to get those reviews.

How to Score 5-Star Reviews

At the conclusion of each stay, guests review their hosts against six criteria, each of which are rated between one to five. Before the guest reviews each of the six criteria, they are asked to rate the **entire stay** out of five:

How was your stay at Thomas's place?
We won't share your responses until after your host writes a review too.

⭐ ⭐ ⭐ ⭐ ⭐

They are then asked to **describe** their trip. When describing their trip, guests are asked the following questions and are provided with the following answer options:

How would you describe the location?

- Central
- Walkable
- Close to public transport
- Secluded
- Close to restaurants and shops
- Close to nightlife

What was the neighborhood like?

- Residential
- Scenic
- Lively
- Quiet
- Hip
- Family-friendly

Did you stay here for any of the following reasons?

- Family travel with children under 2
- Family travel with children under 2-12
- Business travel
- None of the above

How would you describe the quality of the home?

- Budget – Limited amenities and minimal furnishing
- Basic – Standard necessities, plain or outdated furnishing
- Comfort – Well-equipped space for a comfortable stay
- Upscale – Beautiful space with high-end amenities and decor

Hosts will only ever see aggregate answers that multiple guests have selected.

Guests are then asked to rate each of the following criteria with a rating between one to five:

- **Accuracy**
- **Check-in**
- **Cleanliness**
- **Communication**
- **Location**
- **Value**

We overview each of these review criteria in greater detail below…

Accuracy

This is a guest's opportunity to shower thanks upon truthful hosts that set honest expectations from the get-go or seek payback for being sold a place different to what they were led to believe they would be walking into.

Under Airbnb's Content Policy, hosts are obliged to create listings that are honest, clear, and helpful to potential guests. Whilst there is nothing wrong with positioning yourself in your best light, the Content Policy does include a prohibition against posting content that is fraudulent, false, misleading or deceptive.

Common sense should be your guide in deciding what constitutes effective "marketing" versus deceptive misrepresentations.

Airbnb guests are not typically looking for cookie-cutter accommodation options. When communicated effectively, accuracy in your listing's unique features and differentiators can actually be transformed into key selling points that elevate your listing and its appeal to guests.

If anything less than 5-stars are given, Airbnb will ask the guest **what were the main issues**. In addition to adding personal details, the guest is able to select from the following issue options:

- Wi-Fi
- Size of home
- Amenities

- Listing description
- Photos
- Noise

Across the different review categories, Airbnb will provide a selection of "issue options" (like the ones above) for the guest to pick from. These represent common issues of particular concern to guests. Therefore pay extra attention to understanding these issue categories *prior* to any of them actually becoming issues for your guests.

Tip #1: Not Everything Will Be Pretty

Even if you have an impressive pad in a great neighborhood with amazing amenities; your place will inevitably possess *some* less-than-desirable features. This is part and parcel of reality.

Bar open downstairs till the wee-hours of the morning? Mattress a little more on the firmer side? Sociable roommate that likes to bring the party home? Call these out early and help guests avoid unwanted surprises. You never know… for many people, these may actually be drawcards for wanting to stay at your place.

Tip #2: Accuracy in Photos too

Include photos that truly help a guest envisage what it would feel like to stay at your place – not just the key features and amenities. Include at least one photo of each room that guests will have access to.

Ensure the place looks its best, but don't dress it up to the extent that guests wonder if they've walked into the right home upon arrival.

Photos are covered in greater detail on page 106 in the *Building the Perfect Listing* chapter.

Tip #3: Thoroughness in Your Listing

Your Airbnb listing is your principal mechanism for providing prospective guests with an insight into what it might be like to stay at your place. They are yet to see it and therefore have only your listing page to go by when making their choice.

An Airbnb listing is comprised of a listing name and summary; overview of the space, areas the guest can access, your interaction with guests, the neighborhood, how to get around and house rules.

Each of these represents an opportunity to provide information with great clarity and accuracy. They also represent an opportunity to mislead guests and provide inaccurate representations. Ensure accuracy prevails in your listing descriptions.

Building a thorough Airbnb listing is covered in greater detail on page 114 in the *Building the Perfect Listing* chapter.

Check-In

The check-in process is arguably the most important criteria to get right for hosts. A warm, frictionless and problem-free check-in will set the tone for the rest of your guest's trip. Getting off on the wrong foot will have the opposite effect and flavor all other elements of the stay in a negative light.

Fortunately, the check-in process happens to be highly repeatable. You're also able to anticipate many guest questions, and the information that would be most helpful to them too.

With all of this in mind, taking a moment to get this right for one set of guests will enable you to simply hit the repeat button with all future guests too – a big reward from a small investment.

If anything less than 5-stars are given, Airbnb will ask the guest **what were the main issues**. In addition to adding personal details, the guest is able to select from the following issue options:

- Directions
- Late host
- Entering the home

The check-in process is covered in greater detail on page 245 in *The Check-In Process* chapter.

Tip #1: Getting Them to Your Place

Helping guests simply get to your place is the first step to a problem-free check-in. Find out how they'll be arriving (flight, rail, bus, driving, etc.) and let them know the easiest way of getting from their arrival point to your place. Ensure they know how to contact you if there are any hiccups to their arrival plans, and ask if there's anything you're able to do to help make their arrival more effortless or comfortable.

Explain the check-in procedure, whether anyone will be there to meet and greet them, and how they're able to get the keys and orient themselves to your place and the surrounding area.

Tip #2: Have Someone Meet Them in Person

It may not always be possible to meet and greet your guests in person upon their arrival at your place. Depending on your motivations for hosting on Airbnb, doing this for each and every guest may represent taking your desired investment in Airbnb further than you have any interest. Despite this, there's no substitute for the warmth and reassurance felt by having a friendly face be there in-person to physically meet and greet you upon arrival.

Guests greatly appreciate having a real person walk them through their temporary home-away-from-home, explain amenities and features in-person and answer any questions they may have. Whenever possible, this is highly preferable and will be rewarded with positive reviews.

Having someone meet and greet your guests in-person is covered in greater detail on Page 248 in *The Check-In Process* chapter.

Tip #3: Create a House Manual

A House Manual explains how amenities and features of your home works. For example, hosts can let their guests know how to turn on the hot water heater or where they can find an extra blanket.

Guests receive this information in an email once they've confirmed a reservation. It's likely that many guests won't review your house manual at the time of booking, and those that do will almost certainly have forgotten the finer details by the time of their stay. Therefore, print off your house manual and leave it as a hard copy too for reference upon check-in or at any other time throughout the booking.

House Manuals eliminate problems by preempting known challenges or questions and ensuring your guests appreciate the full range of amenities and home features available to them. House Manuals leave guests feeling confident and content from the get-go – a sentiment likely to be carried throughout the rest of their stay too.

House manuals are covered in greater detail on page 259 in the *Providing a Phenomenal Guest Experience* chapter.

Cleanliness

One of Airbnb's Hospitality Standards is cleanliness. Providing a clean and tidy space will make your guests feel comfortable from the moment they arrive as well as show your commitment to making them feel at home and welcome.

You have the ability to add a cleaning fee to your listing price. If you can't (or don't want to) do the cleaning yourself, you can always hire a professional cleaning service.

If anything less than 5-stars are given, Airbnb will ask the guest **what were the main issues.** In addition to adding personal details, the guest is able to select from the following issue options:

- Bathroom
- Bugs
- Towels and linens
- Dust
- Kitchen
- Floors and carpet
- Odors
- Shower

Tip #1: Welcome Guests to a Clean Home

Many guests have traveled great distances to finally arrive at your place. The last thing a paying guest wants to walk into is a messy place. It may seem obvious, but clean every room that your guests can access throughout their stay. Pay special attention to bedrooms, bathrooms and the kitchen. Make sure towels and linens are freshly-washed.

Tip #2: It's Often the 'Small Things'

Take care of the small things that show extra consideration: Dust the bookshelves, wipe the mirrors, empty the wastebasket and make room in the closet or dresser so that guests can store their belongings.

These things may feel like they'll go unnoticed, but are likely to be remembered upon reflection precisely because it's often the small things that get remembered the most.

Tip #3: Give Yourself Enough Time

Ensure that you give yourself enough time to clean your space, particularly when you have back-to-back bookings. Giving your guests the ability to tidy up after themselves will be a big help, so be sure to leave cleaning products at your place to enable guests to take care of spills and accidental messes.

An overview of what needs to be cleaned with each turnover is covered on page 284 in the *Check-Out, Cleaning and Turnover* chapter.

Communication

Most hosts think about communication being important only in terms of their responsiveness to booking inquiries and reservation requests. Whilst definitely important, this represents only the *beginning* of good communication between you and your guest.

Whether it's in solving specific problems, providing general advice, or simply letting guests know how to operate the TV; remember that as an Airbnb host, you adopt the role of a hotel concierge when it comes to maximizing the ease and enjoyment of your guests' trips.

You therefore need to remain contactable, communicative and helpful at all times throughout your guest's stay.

If anything less than 5-stars are given, Airbnb will ask the guest **what were the main issues**. In addition to adding personal details, the guest is able to select from the following issue options:

- Host unreachable
- Check-in arrangements

Tip #1: Maximize the Ways they're Able to Contact You

Let guests know how you're able to be contacted throughout their stay. Are you happy for them to email you? SMS you? Call you?

A natural reluctance of hosts is the fear that opening too many channels of communication is an invitation for being inundated with problems left, right and center. The reality is the opposite.

Guests are typically either focused on utilizing their limited travel time for best use, or reluctant to bother their hosts unnecessarily. And sometimes simply providing an answer to a basic question over a call will avoid a long and drawn-out game of email or SMS "ping-pong" – thus actually saving you time and inconveniencing you less.

A great way to establish the multitude of communication channels available to guests is in the *Interaction with Guests* section of your Airbnb listing. You can see a best practice example of this on page 121 in the *Building the Perfect Listing* chapter.

In addition to explaining all of the communication channels available to guests, you also increase the likelihood of coming across as a great host and receiving additional bookings as a result.

Tip #2: Notify Guests of Unexpected Changes

If something about your place has changed since the time you confirmed a reservation, communicate it in advance to your guests. Guests are much more likely to be understanding when given foreknowledge.

If the change is substantial, offer practical suggestions for ways you may be able to provide a temporary remedy or partially compensate for the inconvenience. Whilst this is also just common courtesy, it will often be seen as going above-and-beyond what was reasonably expected.

Tip #3: Proactively Check In Periodically

There's nothing more comforting than receiving an email or SMS from your host that simply asks how everything's going and if there's anything they're able to do to make the stay more enjoyable. Being proactively communicative will be a welcome surprise for your guest, and stand out in their memory upon reflection of their trip.

Remember too that guests may often feel that their "problem", "issue" or "concern" is too minor to warrant contacting their hosts about, so being a host that gets on the front-foot and asks their guests about anything that would improve their stay will be a welcomed gesture.

Location

It may seem somewhat unfair that location is one of the review criteria that you're scored against. A natural objection is that your place is simply located where it is located, and there's little you're able to do about that. Logic would suggest that a place in a less-than-desirable location will simply charge less in recognition of this fact. Whilst all of this is true, guests have a keen interest in staying in prime locations.

Doing a few simple things will go a great distance in bringing out the best your local area has to offer, helping guests avoid the places they'd most likely want to avoid, and assisting them in getting around to everywhere they'd likely want to go.

If anything less than 5-stars are given, Airbnb will ask the guest to explain why with personal details.

Tip #1: Create a Guidebook

The easiest way to let guests know about the best your local area has to offer is with a local area guidebook. Guidebooks let hosts suggest great local spots like restaurants, grocery stores, parks, and attractions.

Guidebooks take the guesswork out of deciding where to go to experience all the sort of things guests are typically interested in. Guidebooks leave guests feeling like they've been provided with insider tips that inevitably leave them feeling like a true local.

Developing a guidebook for your listing is covered in greater detail on page 262 in the *Providing a Phenomenal Guest Experience* chapter.

Tip #2: Use Your Airbnb Listing

When guests feel like a "local" they naturally form a personal affinity towards the local area. And this affinity means they're more likely to view the location favorably upon reflection.

Your Airbnb listing provides a section for overviewing your neighborhood. Use this section to highlight your neighborhood's key selling points and proximity to places of interest, key landmarks, attractions and public transport.

See a best practice example of this on page 124 in the *Building the Perfect Listing* chapter.

Tip #3: Recommend Public Transport Options

Your guests will almost certainly want to leave your immediate local area at some point throughout their stay. Providing them with clear instructions on the various public transport options available to them will help reinforce the impression that your place is situated in a convenient spot.

You're able to do this on your Airbnb listing in the *Getting Around* section. See a best practice example of this on page 125 in the *Building the Perfect Listing* chapter.

Value

Just like location, value is a highly subjective concept. What you charge will likely be a key determinant on perceptions of value by guests: At $100 a night, maybe your place would be considered lacking in value, but at $50 a night it may be considered a steal. Unfortunately, perceptions of value will differ from guest-to-guest and there isn't much you can do to overcome variance in expectations between guests.

However it isn't just your nightly rate that establishes value. If anything, guests are unlikely to have booked somewhere that they didn't feel provided value for money at the time that they booked it. This represents an opportunity to demonstrate value in a variety of other ways too. With small but smart tricks, you're able to win over even the harshest of critics and leave guests feeling like they've hit the jackpot in finding your place.

If anything less than 5-stars are given, Airbnb will ask the guest to explain why with personal details.

Tip #1: A Few Little Touches Go a Long Way

Airbnb guests are typically not the type of travelers looking for "just another" travel accommodation option. They are discerning travelers wanting a one-of-a-kind experience with personalized touches. Great Airbnb hosts frequently go the extra mile and provide additional amenities and value-adds for their guests.

These are often small, inexpensive things such as a welcome basket of snacks, chocolates on the pillow, basic toiletries and beauty products or complementary tickets to the cinema or a local tourist attraction.

Tip #2: Provide Future Discounts

Since value is so inextricably linked to price, offering guests Special Offer discounts for future stays will boost perceptions of value for their current stay, irrespective of whether they end up taking you up on the offer or not in the future. Offering something as small as a 5% discount on any future stay, or one free night for any future stay over a week will not only increase the perception of value, but may also assist with gaining additional future bookings too.

Tip #3: Send a Thank-You Note

Remember that guests are not obliged to complete the review process. For less-than-desirable guests, this may be a good thing. But many guests simply forget to leave reviews which can be a real pity if they had only good things to say.

Sending a thank-you email immediately after the stay is not only a great reminder to leave a review, but also a reminder of what was hopefully a great experience with an equally-great host – all of which reinforce intrinsic value.

An example thank-you note can be seen on page 244 in the *Booking Acceptance and Communicating With Guests* chapter.

The Remainder of the Review Process

Once the six review criteria have been completed, guests are then given the option of adding a **private note** to their hosts. Here guests are able to offer suggestions for small improvements or say thanks for being a great host.

Finally, the guest is asked to leave their **written review**. This is a *public* review and will live on the host's Airbnb listing page as well as also being viewable from the host's profile. Below is an example review:

Juliet

This is a roomy apartment in a great spot. Lovely cafe and other restaurants right below making dinner quick and easy. We stayed with two adults and two young children and easily had enough space for all of us. Thomas is an attentive host and is keen to ensure you have a great stay. I would definitely stay here again when coming back to New York!

February 2017 ·

ᕦ Helpful

Use both the public review and private feedback you receive as an opportunity to make improvements to your listing or the hospitality you provide.

Leaving Reviews

Leaving a review for your guest is a chance to show your gratitude and provide helpful feedback. Because they're public, your reviews help other hosts know what to expect when they receive a reservation request from a guest who has stayed at your place before.

Rate & review Juliet's group

Family-friendly Dream NYC Apartment
Jul 15 – 18, 2017

Describe Your Experience (required)
Your review will be public on your guest's profiles.

> What was it like to host these guests?

500 words left

Private Guest Feedback
This feedback is just for your guests. We won't make it public.

> Thank your guests for visiting or offer some tips to help them improve for their next trip.

Cleanliness
Did the guests leave your space clean?

★★★★★

Communication
How clearly did the guests communicate their plans, questions, and concerns?

★★★★★

Observance of House Rules
Did the guests observe the house rules you provided?

★★★★★

Would you recommend these guests?
Your answer will not be posted on your profile or your guests' profiles.

👎 No   👍 Yes!

Submit

The "Blind" Review System

The Airbnb review system is a "blind" review – meaning that both hosts and guests do not need to worry about "retribution" negative reviews if they give negative reviews to the other.

Neither the guest nor host knows how the other party have reviewed them until both parties have reviewed one another or the two-week window for providing a review has closed.

Giving Feedback

If you have constructive feedback for a guest, you're able to share this feedback with them either through your **public review** or through **private feedback.** Just like you, most guests will appreciate receiving constructive feedback in a private message, unless it's something you believe other Airbnb hosts should be made aware of.

Here's an example of private feedback that was provided by a guest during the review process and is only visible to the host:

> 🔒 **Private Feedback:**
> Hi Thomas. Thank you for hosting me and my family. Our stay was great. Unfortunately we had trouble accessing the rooftop with the keys you gave us. We eventually got it, but you might want to check if the locks need replacing.

Timing

You have 14 days to complete your review after a trip has ended.

You'll only see the guest's review from a completed trip after *both* you and your guest have left a review, or at the end of the 14-day review period – whichever comes first.

Within 24-hours of your guest's check-out, you will be sent an email reminder to leave a review of your guest:

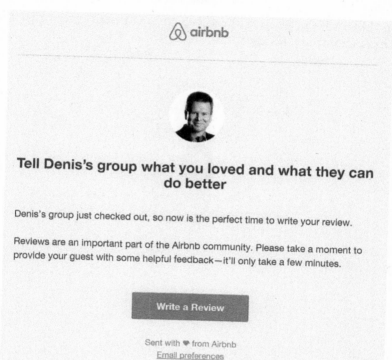

You're encouraged to send a thank you note too that mentions your positive review of them and a request for them to reciprocate in kind should they have had a good time staying at your place.

Being Strategic When Things Went Well

Clever hosts use the timing of when they leave their reviews as a strategic tactic for increasing the likelihood of receiving positive reviews.

The more time that passes between a guest's stay and their submission of a review, the less likely they are to remember all the little things that they enjoyed. Moreover, the less time that passes, the more likely they are to explain in great detail and specificity all of the things they enjoyed throughout their stay.

Therefore, when a problem-free trip has finished, ensure that you submit your review of your guest as soon as possible.

Upon doing so, the guest will receive an email notification that their host has submitted a review:

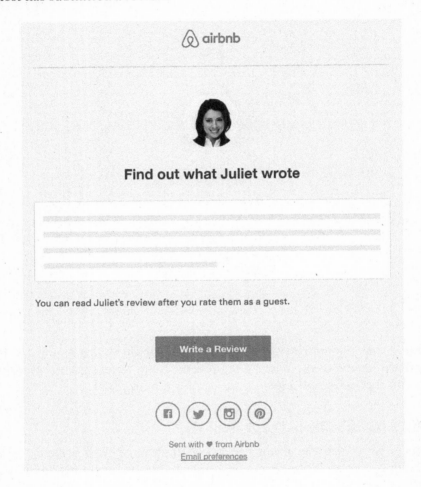

Many guests will also be intrigued to find out what you had to say about them, and the only way they're able to find that out (without waiting out the 14 day review window) is to submit a review of their own.

Being Strategic When Things Didn't Go Well

Clever hosts also appreciate that the opposite also applies when leaving reviews.

If there were problems or any obvious dissatisfaction by your guest, the smart thing to do is to not submit a review at least until the guest has done so themselves. This way, you will not trigger the automated notification being sent to the guest that tells them you've completed your review of them, to which they will then likely complete their (negative) review of you.

Your best hope is that they will simply forget to review you at all and consequentially help you "dodge a bullet".

Leaving a Public Response to Reviews Received

You can't change or remove a review you receive from a guest that you've hosted. Nonetheless, both you and your guests have two weeks to **respond** to any review that you do receive. Your response will appear on your listing page directly below the review it relates to.

Ensure that you respond to all reviews – both good and bad.

Responding to Positive Reviews

When you respond to a positive review, thank the guest for their kind words, and make mention of a few small details that you enjoyed about hosting them. Let the guest know that they're always welcome back at your place:

 Ryan Stayed here for one week and could not have asked for a better place to stay! Thomas is a great host – any problems or questions were resolved straight away. I would highly recommend Thomas and his place to anyone looking for a great place to stay.

 Response from Thomas:
Thanks Ryan. It was a pleasure hosting you and your group. Hope you make it back again soon - you're welcome at the apartment anytime!

These small gestures will demonstrate your good nature, and further reinforce the positive review for all other prospective guests considering booking your place too.

Responding to Negative Reviews

When you respond to a negative review, focus on simply rebutting the specific issues the guest has raised that would otherwise tarnish your good reputation.

For example, you may wish to explain anything that happened that was outside of your control and any remedial measures you took to address a problem that the guest failed to mention.

Don't get swept up in a nasty, petty or bitter *who-did-what-to-whom* debate – whether right or wrong, you won't come across favorably in the eyes of prospective guests who are yet to meet you.

Simply state your case, and leave it at that. If you're lucky and do this right, it may even represent an opportunity to show off your maturity and how you're the type of the host that won't get swept up in personal or petty attacks whilst still demonstrating your commitment to satisfying your guests and the Airbnb community.

Getting Paid and Tax Time

Getting Paid on Airbnb

Airbnb have a dedicated payment system that facilitates all payments according to a process that provides flexibility and financial security to hosts and guests. Airbnb's dedicated payment system ensures safe and secure collection of payment from guests to guarantee payment. All Airbnb bookings need to be paid for via this system.

Part of the success of Airbnb has been the simplification of the payment transaction processes between host and guest. No longer do either party need to worry about getting paid or how to facilitate those payments.

The Airbnb payment process empowers hosts to select their preferred payout method(s) and then automates the nominated payout process.

Below is an outline of the various stages of the Airbnb payout process, and all the things you should be familiar with at each of those stages:

1. Host selects **payout method**
2. **Guest pays** Airbnb when they book a place
3. Airbnb **calculates the payout**
4. Airbnb **release money** to hosts after guest checks-in
5. Host **receives funds**

Payments outside the system are a breach of Airbnb's Terms of Service, and will result in both parties voiding their protections under Airbnb's cancellation policies, the Guest Refund Policy and other safeguards.

Step 1: Select Payout Method

Airbnb offer five methods of receiving payment. You can have multiple methods and use routing rules to split your payouts amongst them. Your payment options include:

1. Direct deposit / Automated Clearing House (ACH)
2. International wire
3. Payoneer bank transfer / Debit card
4. PayPal
5. Western Union

Here are a few important things to keep in mind when deciding your preferred payout method:

- **Direct Deposit / ACH:** Have your check-book handy to enter your routing number and account number. Make sure to enter the routing number for ACH / direct deposit (and not for international wires). Wait for a small deposit to confirm your account is ready.
- **International Wire:** Depending on your location, you may need to enter your account number or IBAN. Your bank can provide you with all the necessary details. Bank fees may apply.
- **Payoneer Bank Transfer / Debit Card:** Enter your name in as it appears on your official ID. Payoneer needs to approve your details before you can receive payouts.
- **PayPal:** Make sure that your account is activated on *PayPal* before adding it as an Airbnb payout method. Your PayPal account is an email address.
- **Western Union:** Enter your full name (first, middle, last) in the Western Union system as it appears on your official ID. Fees apply.

Adding a Payout Method

Hosts have the choice of how they wish to receive their Airbnb payouts.

Not all payout methods are offered in every location. Hosts are able to select from the above payout methods, which may be offered in full or only partially depending on their location.

To add a payout method:

1. Login to Airbnb
2. Click on your account profile photo in the top right corner
3. Select **Account Settings**
4. Click **Payout Preferences** from the menu on the left
5. Available payout methods and currencies differ by country. Click **Add Payout Method** and enter your address to see the payout options available to you

---

Add Payout Method

Country

| United States | ▾ |

Address Line 1

Address Line 2

City

State / Province

| Alabama | ▾ |

ZIP Code / Postal Code

Next

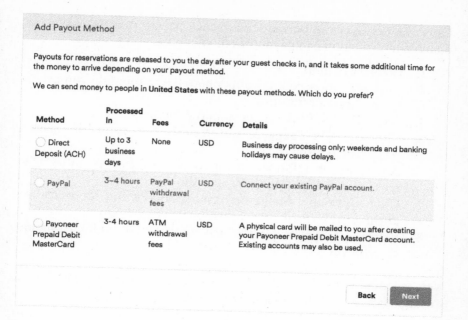

Routing Rules

You can have multiple payout methods and use routing rules to split your payouts amongst them. Routing rules let you split your payouts amongst different payout methods or set a different payout method for each listing in your account.

To use routing rules, you will first need to add more than one payout method.

Once you've added additional payout methods, from **Payout Preferences**, scroll down to **Payout Routing Rules** and click **Add Payout Routing Rule**.

When you add a new payout routing rule, only payouts for reservations that begin after the rule has been added will be affected. The payout method for reservations that have already begun will remain unchanged.

If you remove a payout method that is included in a routing rule, the associated routing rule will no longer be valid.

Only one taxpayer can be assigned to each payout method. To assign taxpayer information to a payout method:

1. Login to Airbnb
2. Click on your account profile photo in the top right corner
3. Select **Account Settings**
4. Select **Payout Preferences** from the menu on the left
5. Click the **Add Taxpayer** button in the **Taxpayer Information** box at the bottom
6. Add taxpayer information for each individual or entity who receives earnings from your account
7. Click **Options** > **Assign taxpayer** in the **Payout Methods** box at the top
8. Select a taxpayer for the payout method under **Assigned to taxpayer**

New payout methods, and those that haven't been assigned to a specific taxpayer will be assigned to the default taxpayer.

Step 2: Guest Pays Airbnb When They Book a Place

A guest's payment information is collected when they submit a reservation request.

If you as the host accept the reservation request, Airbnb will then charge the guest's nominated payment method for the entire amount at that time (if your guest is staying for longer than 28 nights, they will be charged a first month down payment and the rest will be collected in monthly installments).

Step 3: Airbnb Calculates the Payout

Airbnb calculate the amount of your payout by adding a variety of guest charges and subtracting a variety of Airbnb fees and taxes:

YOUR PAYOUT =		RECIPIENT OF FUNDS	WHEN CHARGED?
Number **x** of nights	Nightly price	Host	**Always**
	+ Extra Guest fee		**Sometimes** – If host specifies an Extra Guest fee and booking meets fee requirement
+ Cleaning fee			**Sometimes** – If host specifies a one-off cleaning fee
- Service fees		Airbnb	**Always** – 3% of total payout
- Currency exchange fee			
x Local taxes		Airbnb (on behalf of government)	**Sometimes** – in specific jurisdictions
- Government-required taxes (e.g. VAT)			

Airbnb Service Fees

There's no such thing as a free lunch, and Airbnb is no different. Airbnb make their money by taking a small fee from hosts and guests. The good news is that at 3%, the fee they take from hosts is significantly smaller than the fee they take from guests (6-12%).

There's also no annual fee for Airbnb, which differentiates it from other major home rental websites such as *HomeAway*, *VRBO* and *VacationRentals.com*.

The 3% service fee includes the nightly rate (x number of nights) as well as the cleaning fee.

As you can see from the following example, the host's Airbnb service fee will be *$12*, calculated as 3% of ($100 x 3 nights) + 3% of the $100 cleaning fee:

Payout		
	$100 x 3 nights	$300
	Cleaning Fees	$100
	Airbnb Service Fee	($12)
	Total Payout	$388

The system only processes whole numbers and will round the fee to the nearest dollar. The Airbnb service fee is deducted from the sub-total (nightly rate x number of nights + cleaning fee) to arrive at the Total Payout.

The service fee that Airbnb will charge to hosts for an upcoming reservation will be displayed on the reservation confirmation email you receive when a guest books.

To view the service fees that Airbnb have charged you for previous reservations:

1. Login to Airbnb
2. Click on your account profile photo in the top right corner
3. Select **Account Settings**
4. Select **Transaction History** (from vertical menu on the left)
5. Click on the alpha-numeric reservation code from any prior reservation

Date	Type	Details	Amount	Paid Out
02-01-2016 ❷	Payout	Transfer to *****1234		$1552
02-01-2016	Reservation	Jan 01 – 04, 2016 ABCDE1FGHI Lauren Smith Family-friendly Dream NYC Apartment	$1552	

The relevant Airbnb reservation itinerary will load and display a payout breakdown exactly like the example at the top of this page.

Step 4: Airbnb Release Money to Host After Guest Checks-In

Airbnb will release the money to hosts 24 hours after the guest checks-in.

If you have a minimum payout amount set, your payout won't be released until that amount is met. If you have multiple listings with check-in's on the same day, any funds going to the same payout method will be deposited as a single payout. And if your guest is staying for longer than 28 nights, payouts for that reservation will be released monthly.

Step 5: Host Receives Funds

The time it takes for the funds to arrive in a host's account depends on their selected payout method. Below are the average processing times for each payout method:

METHOD	TIME FOR PAYOUT
ACH / Direct deposit	Up to 3 business days
Bank Transfer / International Wire	3 – 7 business days
PayPal	Within 1 business day
Western Union	1 business day (US Pacific Time)
Payoneer Prepaid Debit Card	Within 1 business day

To check the status of a payout, visit your **Transaction History**. Once Airbnb have sent your payout, a "Payout" line item appears for that reservation:

Completed Transactions	Future Transactions	Gross Earnings			

Paid out: $1,000   Earnings Summary | Export to CSV

All payout metho ▼	All listings ▼	2017 ▼	From: January ▼	To: December ▼

Date	Type	Details	Amount	Paid Out
01-02-2017	Payout	Transfer to Account *****1234		$600
02-01-2017	Reservation	Feb 1 – 3, 2017 FG2HIJ Adam Smith Family-friendly Dream NYC Apartment	$600	
03-02-2017 ❔	Payout	Transfer to Account *****1234		$400
01-01-2017	Reservation	Jan 1 – 2, 2017 AB1CDE Natalie Mayor Family-friendly Dream NYC Apartment	$400	

Many banking systems don't process transactions on weekends or holidays. If your payout from Airbnb is completed between Friday and Sunday, it might not be processed until the following week.

Airbnb will send you an email notification to advise that the funds have been transferred via your nominated payout method:

⌂ airbnb

Hi Thomas,

We've issued you a payout of $1000 via Bank Transfer. This payout should arrive in your account by Sep 1, 2017, taking into consideration weekends and holidays.

Date	Detail	Amount
08/27/2017 – 08/31/2017	ABCD12EFGH – Michael Smith	$1000

You can view the status of your payouts in your transaction history.

Thanks,
The Airbnb Team

Airbnb and Taxes

Despite being a lucrative goldmine of opportunity, with profit comes the taxman. And whilst none of us are excited about saying farewell to a portion of our hard-earned profits, the alternative can be much worse: audits, avoidable legal and accounting expenses and infuriating headaches.

Tax authorities are still grappling with how to tax the "sharing economy", and the sand is yet to set in a way that provides a level of certainty that hosts are looking for in maximizing their profitability whilst minimizing their tax obligations.

However, gaining a basic understanding of how to navigate your tax responsibilities on Airbnb as well as understanding ways to maximize legitimate tax deductions is still within your reach.

To begin with, let's run through some Accounting 101: Tax obligation = tax dues – tax deductions. But what are the applicable Airbnb tax dues owed and what deductions can you make for Airbnb expenses incurred?

Well, when it comes to Airbnb...
Your **tax obligation =**

Income Taxes	+	**Local Taxes**	+	**Value Added Taxes**

–	**Full Deductions**	–	**Partial Deductions**

Not all taxes will be applicable to everyone, and different hosts are entitled to different deductions. It is important to be familiar with each to understand your personal circumstances and tax obligations.

The following pages contain a run through of each of these elements and the things you need to be familiar with to maximize your Airbnb earning potential.

Before diving into it, it's important to remember that tax advice is complicated, and you should do your own due diligence when receiving advice. Airbnb hosts should consult a tax professional for assistance in reporting their income.

Income Taxes

Tax Information you Provide to Airbnb

Every Airbnb host with a U.S. listing is required to specify their **U.S. tax status.** Non-U.S. Airbnb hosts with listings outside the U.S. are not required to specify their U.S. tax status.

To specify your U.S. tax status:

1. Login to Airbnb
2. Click on your account profile photo in the top right corner
3. Select **Settings**
4. Select **Payout Preferences** from the menu on the left
5. Click the **Add taxpayer** button under the **Taxpayer Information**

Below is a summary of each of the options you're able to select:

1. **U.S. Person or Entity**

   IRS Substitute Form Provided to Airbnb: **W-9**

   Whilst not obligatory to complete or return the W-9 form to Airbnb, failure to do so will result in Airbnb withholding 28% from your payouts which they will automatically remit to the IRS. In the event that this occurs, the amount remitted will be noted on *Form 1099-K (see next page).*

2. **Non-U.S. Person *with* a U.S. Taxpayer ID Number**

   IRS Substitute Form Provided to Airbnb: **W-8ECI**

   As a withholding agent, Airbnb is required to receive the W-8ECI form. Failure to provide this form to Airbnb will result in them withholding a mandatory 28% from your payouts which they will remit to the IRS.

3. **Non-U.S. Person *without* a U.S. Taxpayer ID Number**

   IRS Substitute Form Provided to Airbnb: **W-8BEN**

   The W-8BEN form is used to confirm your foreign status. Airbnb will automatically withhold 30% on all payouts from U.S. listings (unless valid tax treaty benefits can be claimed). In the event that this occurs, the amount remitted will be noted on *Form 1042-S (see next page).*

Tax Forms Provided to You From Airbnb

Depending on your account status, the taxpayer information you've submitted to Airbnb, and other factors, you may receive a tax form from Airbnb. Below is a summary of the different categories to whom Airbnb will issue tax forms:

1. **U.S. persons who have earned over $20,000 and had 200+ reservations**

   Tax Form Provided by Airbnb: **1099-K**

   Any Form 1099-K issued to you will be available in your *Payout Preferences.* You'll receive an email notification when your form is ready, typically in late January of each year. Airbnb will also mail a copy to the address you provided along with your taxpayer information, unless you opted for electronic delivery only. You may receive more than one Form 1099-K if your taxpayer information is listed on multiple Airbnb accounts.

2. **Non-U.S. persons who have submitted a Form W-8**

   Tax Form Provided by Airbnb: **1042-S**

   Hosts with U.S.-sourced earnings who have submitted a Form W-8 will be provided a Form 1042-S. Hosts receive a Form 1042-S in the mail at the address they entered when submitting their tax information, typically in late February of each year.

3. **Hosts that had taxes withheld from their payouts**

   Tax Form Provided by Airbnb: *Varies*

   If taxes were withheld from payouts during the calendar year (applies to both U.S. and non-U.S. hosts), these hosts will be provided with the appropriate tax form so that they may account for the withholdings on their income tax return.

   If you received a request to submit your taxpayer information and haven't provided it to Airbnb, they may be required to withhold 28% from your payouts and remit the withholdings to the U.S. Internal Revenue Service (IRS). You can avoid this by submitting your taxpayer information.

Once Airbnb receive your information, they won't withhold from your future payouts (however, any amounts that have already been withheld and remitted to the IRS cannot be returned to you by Airbnb). The total amount withheld will be included on any tax forms issued to you so that you may account for these withholdings on your income tax return.

If you think you've submitted the wrong information, you can always make updates to the **taxpayer information** you provide to Airbnb. Airbnb encourage hosts to consult a tax professional for assistance in reporting their income.

Local Taxes

Local taxes go by many names. Some of the more common names are:

- Occupancy Tax
- Lodging Tax
- Room Tax
- Sales Tax
- Tourist Tax
- Hotel Tax

It is a tax that is assessed and levied by a local authority such as a city, state or country. Not every locality will have applicable local taxes, however many do.

Where they exist, they typically apply to rentals of 30 or fewer days, and average 12% of the rental revenue. In many instances, hosts are required to register with their local city or county. Sometimes, a business licence will also be required before collecting local taxes.

It is therefore important to familiarize yourself with any local taxes that may exist within your area. The best way to do this is to check your city or county government website.

Airbnb take responsibility for collecting local taxes on behalf of hosts only in specific locations. Currently, these include **France, India, Mexico, Netherlands, Portugal, Switzerland** and the **United States** (with the exception of Delaware, Georgia, Hawaii, Indiana, Iowa, Kentucky, Massachusetts, Mississippi, Missouri, Montana, Nebraska, New Hampshire, North Dakota, Ohio, South Dakota, West Virginia and Wyoming).

The Airbnb website (**www.airbnb.com/help/article/653**) has detailed information on the relevant local taxes it collects for each of these locations.

For hosts required to collect local taxes in any location that is *not* listed above, it is their responsibility to collect the local tax direct from guests themselves.

These taxes may be due monthly, quarterly or yearly depending on the governing area's requirements. In some instances, filing of taxes, even in the absence of rental income, may be required for reporting purposes once registered.

If your listing falls within any of the jurisdictions previously listed, an "Occupancy Taxes" line item will be displayed on your Airbnb listing page:

If you are required to collect local taxes and do not live within any of the jurisdictions listed on the previous page, it is *your* responsibility to collect these taxes from your guests.

Hosts have three options for doing so, and it is at the discretion of hosts as to how they wish to collect these taxes. Their options are:

1. Incorporating them into their listing's nightly price
2. Adding it to a Special Offer
3. Asking guests to pay it in person upon arrival

Whilst the obligation is for the guest to pay any applicable local taxes, the onus is still on the host to remit these funds to the local taxing authority (when not collected by Airbnb on the host's behalf). Regardless of the method elected, hosts are required to inform guests of the exact amount they will be paying in local taxes prior to booking.

In some circumstances, exceptions for reservations over a certain number of nights will eliminate the need to collect any relevant local taxes. You should research and familiarize yourself with any circumstances that might apply to you.

Value Added Tax (VAT)

Valued Added Tax (or VAT) is a tax assessed on the supply of goods and services. In Japan, Japanese Consumption Tax, or JCT, is applicable instead of VAT. In Australia and New Zealand, Goods and Services Tax (GST), is applicable instead of VAT. Depending on the laws of your local jurisdiction, VAT may also be included as a tax deduction in addition to the 3% service fee.

Airbnb charges VAT on its service fees for customers from Albania, Iceland, Norway, Russia, Serbia, South Africa, Switzerland, Taiwan, the Bahamas, and the European Union. In Japan, JCT will apply, and in Australia and New Zealand, GST will apply. If you live in one of these countries (where Airbnb charge VAT on their service fees), then VAT, JCT and GST rates are calculated according to the local rate of the host's country of residence. Hosts from all other countries are responsible for self-assessing any relevant VAT that might be owed.

The service fee presented to you by Airbnb will include VAT when applicable. VAT or GST is deducted from your payout and is based on the total host service fee for a reservation. If you change your reservation, VAT or GST adjusts to reflect any change in the service fee.

A VAT invoice is provided whenever VAT is assessed on Airbnb service fees. An invoice is finalized and issued when a reservation is accepted, and includes your information (name, address, etc.) as you entered it in your Airbnb account. Airbnb is not able to modify a VAT invoice after it has been issued. To access the VAT invoice for your reservation:

1. Login to Airbnb
2. In **Hosting** mode, scroll down to **Reservations** on your hosting dashboard and select **View all reservations**
3. Find the relevant reservation. If the reservation you're looking for isn't displayed, click **View all reservation history**
4. Select **View VAT Invoices** under the **Details** column
5. Select **Host Invoice**

If you have a VAT ID number registered with the European Commission, you may want to associate that number with your Airbnb account (this option is not available in Ireland). This will include your VAT ID on Airbnb VAT invoices created after the VAT ID is added.

To provide a valid VAT Information Exchange System (VIES) ID number for your account:

1. Login to Airbnb
2. Click on your account profile photo in the top right corner
3. Select **Profile**
4. Select **Edit Profile** (next to profile picture)
5. Select **Add VAT ID Number** under **Optional**
6. Enter your VAT ID number verification information
7. Click **Verify**
8. Click **Save**

When your VAT ID number is successfully verified by the European Commission, you won't be charged VAT on Airbnb's service fees. It nonetheless remains your responsibility to self-assess whether you need to pay VAT for the use of Airbnb's services.

If your VAT ID number can't be verified and you determine that you do need to self-assess VAT on Airbnb's service fees, Airbnb encourage you to consult a tax advisor for assistance.

Deductions

Tax deductions for Airbnb hosts fall into one of two categories:

1. **Full Deductions** are expenses incurred solely for the purposes of running your Airbnb operation. An example is the purchase of linen for the bed in a room used exclusively for Airbnb guests.

2. **Partial Deductions** are expenses incurred for the shared purposes and benefits of yourself and Airbnb guests. They arise in instances where an Airbnb dwelling is either rented out on a part-time basis (with you or others living there the remainder of the time), or where only part of your space is rented out (with you or others living in the rest of the space too).

The distinction in deduction type is important as it determines the size of the deduction you're able to claim for individual expenses.

Full Deductions

Below are some common larger expenses you're able to claim as full deductions:

- **Airbnb Host Fees:** The 3% hosting fee you pay to Airbnb is entirely deductible. To determine how much you've paid in host fees login to your Airbnb account, go to *Host > Transaction History*, click on *Export to CSV* (in the top right-hand corner), and sum the amounts in the *Host Fee* column)

- **Guest amenities:** These include things like toiletries, spa products or anything you've provided for your guests to enhance their experience

- **Guest bedding and linen:** Bedding, linen and towels for guests are entirely tax-deductible

- **Food for guests:** Make sure that deductions claimed for food purchased for guests is separate from food that you've purchased for yourself

- **Mileage for conducting Airbnb activity:** If you manage multiple listings, or drive your guests places as part of your service (e.g. airport pick-up's / drop-off's) then these expenses will be entirely deductible. Check the applicable dollar-per-mile allowance that applies within your local jurisdiction

This list covers some full-deduction expenses, but is far from exhaustive. Other fully-deductible expenses may exist for your listing. To determine whether a particular expense qualifies as a full deduction, use the test: *Was the expense for the exclusive benefit of my guests and connected to the service I provide as an Airbnb host?*

Partial Deductions

Remember selecting what kind of place you are listing when first setting up your listing? This was where you specified whether you were renting out your *entire home*, a *private room* or simply some *shared space*.

Partial tax deductions exist where the expense incurred provides benefit to both *you* and *your guests*.

Both the amount of **space** you rent out of your home as well as the amount of **time** you rent your home for will determine just how much of a deduction you're able to claim.

There are three scenarios where partial deductions may be claimed. Here is a summary of the formula for each:

	Part-Time Rental	Full-Time Rental
Shared Room	$ × 📏 × 📅	$ × 📏
Private Room		
Entire Home	$ × 📅	*Full* deduction

$ Airbnb Expense Incurred   📏 Proportion of Home Rented   📅 Proportion of Year Rented

Let's also take a look at how to determine the partial deduction that's applicable for each...

1. Entire Home + Part-Time Rental

When you rent out your entire place on a part-time basis and live in it for the remainder of the time.

Sample Scenario: Hosts who rent their entire home for a whole month while overseas on vacation

Formula: Expense x Proportion of Year Rented (**$** x 📅)

Example: If yearly rent is $1000 and throughout the year you rented your entire place for 30 nights, then the deduction = $1000 x (30/365) = $82.19

2. Shared / Private Room + Full-Time Rental

When you rent out a shared / private room on a full-time basis but still live in your home the entire time too.

Sample Scenario: Hosts who live year-round in their home but also offer an entire room of that home to Airbnb guests year-round too

Formula: Expense x Proportion of Home Rented (**$** x 📏)

Example: If yearly rent is $1000, you live in a 100 square foot apartment and offer Airbnb guests a 25 square foot space within your apartment, then the deduction = $1,000 x (25/100) = $250

3. Shared / Private Room + Part-Time Rental

When you rent out a shared / private room on a part-time basis but still live in your home the entire time.

Sample Scenario: Hosts who list a room within their apartment on Airbnb and otherwise use that space for other purposes in the absence of hosting Airbnb guests

Formula: Expense x Proportion of Year Rented x Proportion of Home Rented (**$** x 📅 x 📏)

Example: If your yearly rent is $1000, you Airbnb your place for 30 nights of the year, and live in an apartment of 100 square feet of which you offer Airbnb guests a 25 square foot area within that space; then the deduction = $1,000 x (30/365) x (25/100) = $20.55

Co-Hosts

Airbnb co-hosts take on hosting responsibilities for your listing and offer extra support whenever you welcome guests to your place.

Adding co-hosts is a simple way to allow family members or trusted friends to help with some of the hosting responsibilities from their own account without needing to give them access to your personal Airbnb account, personal details, or payment information.

When you add a co-host to your listing, you enable them to accept, decline, cancel, or alter reservations. They are able to see and respond to guest messages. They can edit pricing and availability, as well as edit your listing descriptions and photos. Co-hosts can also interact with Airbnb customer service on your behalf. Below is a summary of the key things an Airbnb co-host can do for you...

Getting your space ready for guests: Your co-host can help prepare your space so it's ready to welcome guests. They can do a little informal interior design and decorations, recommend repairs to prepare the space, purchase necessary items, create a list of supplies to be restocked after each guest stay (e.g. soap, toilet paper, etc.), setup a lockbox, create a house manual, and more.

Listing your space: Your co-host can create a listing for your place on Airbnb. They can help with writing listing descriptions, coming up with an appealing listing name, taking and uploading photos, and help with determining the optimal pricing for your place.

Messaging with guests: Your co-host can message guests on your behalf. Your co-host will communicate with guests using their own Airbnb account to get to know guests, answer questions they may have and coordinate the guest's arrival and departure.

Handling reservations: Your co-host can handle reservations by responding to booking inquiries and accepting or declining reservation requests in a timely manner.

Welcoming guests in person: Your co-host can welcome or coordinate in-person guest check-in's for you. You can ask your co-host to meet your guests in-person (or you can provide access to your home via alternative options).

Responding to guest issues: Your co-host can help handle guest-related travel issues for you. Guests might lock themselves out, the shower may stop working or the internet may go down. Your co-host can jump in at any time to help with the unexpected.

Reviewing guests: Your co-host can review your guests and leave feedback on your behalf.

Updating calendar and pricing: Your co-host can update your calendar and pricing. Keeping your listing's availability up-to-date is important so that guests know when they can book your place. Your co-host can help you decide whether to set prices manually or use Airbnb's Smart Pricing tools.

Re-stocking essential supplies: Your co-host can help stock your place with a few basic guest necessities (like towels, toilet paper and soap) based on an agreed frequency of hosting and purchasing, and with an understanding of how expenses are going to be handled.

Coordinating cleaning and linens: Your co-host can coordinate the cleaning and turnover of your space for you. You may choose to clean your place yourself, or alternatively, work with a cleaning service.

Coordinating maintenance: Your co-host can coordinate repairs for you. If something needs a fix, you and the co-host can determine what repairs are needed, when the repairs should take place, and how any relevant expenses will be handled.

Interacting with Airbnb: Your co-host can contact Airbnb to report and work towards the resolution of any issues you or your guests have during their stay.

Co-hosts can't access your payout information or personal details. As the listing owner, you can remove a co-host at any time.

You can pay your co-hosts for their help by sharing a percentage of your booking earnings. In many instances, a co-host will be responsible for coordinating or undertaking the cleaning – you can automatically route the cleaning fees to your co-hosts for this.

Guests will see your co-hosts' picture and contact information on your listing page, their Airbnb reservation itinerary, and in all messages sent from the co-host's account. This becomes especially useful when your co-host is responsible for most of the guest communications and interactions.

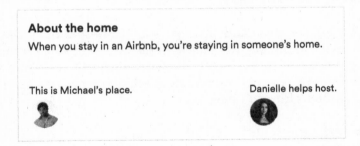

About the home

When you stay in an Airbnb, you're staying in someone's home.

This is Michael's place.

Danielle helps host.

At all times, your co-hosts will be using their own Airbnb accounts – you do not need to share a username, password or profile. This means that when you or your co-hosts message a guest, the guest will know exactly who it is they're talking to.

You're also able to designate your co-host as the *primary* host for your listing. This means they become the main point of contact for guests, both before and during their stay. Guests will see the primary host whenever they look at your listing online and will then expect most of their interactions to be with the primary host during their stay.

Thomas Smith
Listing admin

Primary Host

Guests will see you whenever they see the listing, and will expect more of their interactions to be with you during their stay. You can change the primary host any time. Learn more

Maria Jones
Your co-host since 1 Jan 2017

Remove

Receiving 25% of booking earnings since 2 Jan 2017

Cleaning fees are paid to Maria

💬 Contact info

👤 Make Maria the primary host

🔀 Turn off shared earnings

📋 View transaction history

To add a co-host:

1. Login to Airbnb
2. In **Hosting** mode, select **Listings** from the top navigation bar
3. Select **Manage listing** for your listing
4. Click on **Co-hosts** from the menu at the top
5. Click the **Invite a friend** button under **Host with a friend**

×

Invite a friend

Email address

maria_jones@gmail.com

If you'd like to share a percentage of your booking earnings with your co-host enter that amount here. You can also choose to have the cleaning fees paid to them if they're responsible for handling cleaning. Learn more

Share of earnings (optional)

25%

Cleaning fees (optional)
☑ Pay cleaning fees to this co-host

☑ **I agree to the** Co-host Terms of Service.

When you add a co-host, they can act on your behalf, you're responsible for actions they take when they're hosting your space.

Invite

Airbnb are also rolling out a *Neighborhood Co-host Program* so local hosts can help host your place if you don't personally know someone who can help you.

These co-hosts can help with as much or as little as you need, and together you can negotiate their service fee for the help they provide.

The program isn't available everywhere just yet however. Currently, it is only available in:

- Australia (Brisbane, Melbourne, Perth and Sydney)
- Canada (Toronto)
- New Zealand (Auckland)
- Ireland (Dublin)
- Japan (Tokyo)
- South Africa (Cape Town)
- UK (Edinburgh and London)
- U.S. (Austin, Boston, Chicago, Denver, Houston, Miami, New Orleans, New York, Philadelphia, Phoenix, San Diego, San Jose, Seattle and Washington DC)

If you're in any of these locations, and looking for some co-hosting assistance on Airbnb, visit **www.airbnb.com/co-hosting** to find a co-host for your place.

Continuous Improvement

Tracking Performance

Airbnb assist hosts to track and measure their performance as well as identify areas they're able to continually improve upon. They do this by sharing dynamic statistics, insights, tips and recommendations on your areas of greatest strength as well as biggest improvement opportunities.

You're able to gain useful intelligence on your Airbnb performance in the **Ratings** and **Views** sections of the **Stats** tab within your Airbnb Dashboard:

These two sections are overviewed below.

Ratings

Aside from leveraging good reviews to win additional bookings, the ratings you receive also provide an insight into how good a job you're doing on Airbnb, and any areas you're able to improve upon. To view these insights:

1. Login to Airbnb
2. In **Hosting** mode, select **Stats** from the top navigation bar
3. Select **Ratings** from the sub-menu bar beneath the main menu bar

You'll be presented with statistics and insights across each of the six different review criteria categories, as well as the overall experience. It will also let you know if any of your recent ratings were less than 5-stars.

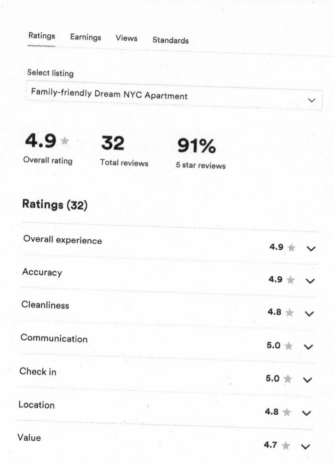

Ratings Earnings Views Standards

Select listing

Family-friendly Dream NYC Apartment ⌄

4.9 ★   **32**   **91%**
Overall rating   Total reviews   5 star reviews

Ratings (32)

Overall experience	4.9 ★	⌄
Accuracy	4.9 ★	⌄
Cleanliness	4.8 ★	⌄
Communication	5.0 ★	⌄
Check in	5.0 ★	⌄
Location	4.8 ★	⌄
Value	4.7 ★	⌄

Clicking on any of the arrows will expand the rating category to reveal additional insights for that category:

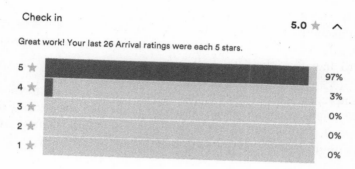

Check in   5.0 ★ ⌃

Great work! Your last 26 Arrival ratings were each 5 stars.

5 ★	97%
4 ★	3%
3 ★	0%
2 ★	0%
1 ★	0%

Views and Bookings

Airbnb also provide you with granular reporting data on the number of **views** your listing has received over the last month as well as on any given day that has passed.

It will also tell you your **booking rate**, which is the percentage of guests that end up booking your place after viewing your listing. Focus less on the specific number, and more on ensuring that your booking rate remains constant or gradually improves.

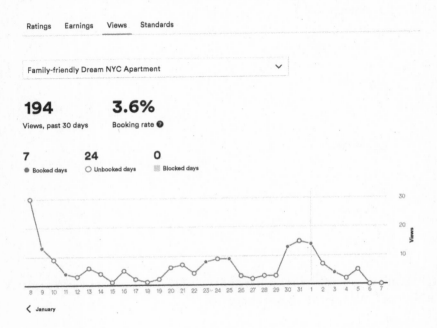

You should continually monitor this data, and track your month-on-month performance. Note changes that take place to infer any insights you might be able to draw from the data.

For example, if your issue is a reduction in *listing views*, it may indicate that you might consider reviewing your strategies for getting found. However, if your issue is a reduction in *reservations*, it may indicate that you might consider improving your listing descriptions.

Let's consider an example of two consecutive sample months:

MONTH	LISTING VIEWS	RESERVATIONS	CONVERSION RATE
July	94	4	4%
August	83	6	7%

By comparing the two months, we're able to note any month-on-month changes as well as identify any conversion "bottlenecks" that are occurring.

Using the example above, some questions that a host may wish to ask themselves would be…

What caused the **reduction in listing views** from July to August?
Was it because…

- They're not **getting found** in search results?
- They're **over-priced**?
- Their **reviews** have gone down?

How did they achieve the **uplift in reservations** from July to August?
Was it because they…

- Reduced their **prices**?
- Gained additional or better **reviews**? (and if so, how?)
- Improved their **listing descriptions** and/or **photos**?

As you can see, these statistics enable you to think like a doctor diagnosing the cause of an illness or identifying the reasons behind improved health.

The majority of Airbnb hosts pay little attention to these insights, nor use them for these diagnostic purposes. This data represents a goldmine of information to assist you in moving beyond simple gut instincts. They enable you to complement your intuition with a data-driven, evidence-based approach for becoming an A+ Airbnb host.

The Secret Ingredient to Becoming an A+ Host

Hosting on Airbnb is not rocket science, but it *is* still something you get better at with time and experience. There's a lot to learn, and a lot to get right. It's easy to feel overwhelmed and confused.

Channel your eagerness for providing superior hospitality experiences into a habit of *continuous improvement.*

All hosts, both new and old, will inevitably make mistakes. The difference between the successful and unsuccessful ones is simply the attitude they adopt in responding to those missteps.

Successful Airbnb hosts begin by embracing the default mindset that they wish to become the best Airbnb hosts they're able to become. When mistakes (inevitably) get made or things don't work out as planned, these hosts reflect upon the lessons they're able to learn and the ways they're able to avoid making those same mistakes the next time round.

By and large, guests recognize the efforts these hosts put into their hospitality standards and endeavours, and respond in-kind. The financial rewards these hosts then receive become the natural by-product of their attitudes, efforts and incremental experience.

For access to additional tips, tools, guides and resources, visit
padlifter.com/resources

Airbnb Documents for Your Review

You may also wish to check out some important documents prepared by Airbnb to help further explain many of the details, technical mechanisms and terms of service described throughout this book.

Below are a list of important Airbnb documents for your review, and a link for accessing them:

Guest Refund Policy Terms:
www.airbnb.com/terms/guest_refund_policy

Host Guarantee Terms and Conditions:
www.airbnb.com/terms/host_guarantee

IP Policy:
www.airbnb.com/terms/copyright_policy

Host Protection Insurance Summary:
www.airbnb.com/users/hpi_program_summary_pdf

Non-discrimination Policy:
www.airbnb.com/terms/nondiscrimination_policy

Payments Terms of Service:
www.airbnb.com/terms/payments_terms

Privacy Policy:
www.airbnb.com/terms/privacy_policy

Terms of Service:
www.airbnb.com/terms

Index

E

F

G

H

hairdryers, 200
headings and bullets, 105, 117, 118, 124
heating, 42, 44, 45, 131, 261
home
  features. *See* amenities
  improvements. *See* maintenance, repairs and renovations
HomeAway, 89, 176, 214, 319
Homeowner's associations, 32, 33, 65
hospitality, 21, 38, 202, 211, 236, 251, 258, 263, 279, 284, 300, 348
  standards. *See* Airbnb hospitality standards
Host Guarantee. *See* Airbnb Host Guarantee
Host Protection Insurance Program. *See* Airbnb Host Protection Insurance Program
hosting
  experience, 87, 91, 155, 165, 192, 196, 197, 199, 202, 210, 294, 348
  frequency, 87, 136
  motivations. See motivations for hosting
hosts
  existing, 19, 20, 21, 87, 210, 348
  new, 19, 20, 21, 74, 87, 146, 155, 156, 197, 210, 211, 291, 294, 348
hot tubs. *See* pools and hot tubs
hotels, 38, 98, 135, 158, 159, 166, 193, 252, 262, 301
house
  manuals, 233, 235, 259, 260, 300
  rules, 32, 35, 75, 85, 86, 126, 127, 128, 129, 130, 131, 194, 220, 233, 298
housing standards. *See* building and housing standards

I

iCalendar, 176
iCloud, 89, 176, 177

ID
  government-issued, 69, 85, 195, 288, 289
  verification process. *See* Airbnb verified ID
importing calendars. *See* calendar importing
income, 25, 26, 28, 34, 62, 98, 134, 137, 163, 282, 283, 294, 327, 328, 338
independent research, 29, 60, 68, 72, 145, 146, 155, 158, 160, 166, 329, 331
injury. *See* bodily injury
inquiries. *See* booking inquiries
insider tips. *See* local knowledge
inspections. *See* property inspections
Instant Book, 75, 94, 191, 192, 193, 194, 196, 197, 198
insurance
  commercial, 55
  companies, 60, 62
  policies, 34, 52, 54, 55, 59, 61, 62, 65
intercoms. *See* buzzers and intercoms
Internal Revenue Service (IRS), 325, 326, 327
international wires, 315
internet and Wi-Fi, 42, 86, 200, 261, 297, *337*
investment, Airbnb as, 28, 29
issues and problems, 33, 35, 49, 66, 71, 128, 131, 187, 230, 236, 237, 243, 251, 255, 258, 260, 277, 297, 299, 300, 301, 302, 303, 311, 312, 337, 338
itineraries, 232, 233, 338

K

key exchange services, 248, 252, 278
keyless access, 45, 200, 247, 248, 250, 252, 253
keys, 172, 200, 247, 252, 253, 254, 255, 260, 278, 299
kids. *See* children
kitchen, 43, 129, 261, 284, 300, 301

L

M

N

O

occupancy
 numbers. *See* number of guests
 rates, 26, 29, 144, 164, 169, 170,
  172, 198, 199, 230, 231
 tax. See taxes, local
odors, 42, 300
Onefinestay, 214
Online Travel Agencies (OTAs), 197,
 214, 319
opportunity. See Airbnb financial
 opportunity
over-charging, 134, 136, 155, 169, 282,
 347
overheads, 130, 164, 230

P

parking, 86, 261, 265
payment information, 85, 194, 318,
 336
payments, 60, 280, 313, 314, 315, 318
Payoneer bank transfers, 315
payout methods, 314, 315, 316, 317,
 318, 321
payouts, 183, 184, 188, 280, 314, 315,
 316, 317, 319, 320, 321, 322, 325,
 338
PayPal, 315
penalties, 30, 33, 126, 190, 191, 198
performance metrics, 204, 344, 346,
 347
permissions, 32, 33
permits, 30, 31
personal
 hygiene products, 42, 200, 258,
  284, 305, 331, 337
 information, 72, 212, 218, 219, 232,
  233, 288, 289, 336, 338
personality, 59, 100, 103, 104, 109, 110,
 114
pets, 51, 83, 86, 200
phone number, 69, 85, 194, 232, 234,
 288, 289
photo captions, 112
photography
 Airbnb professional, 107, 109
 equipment, 82, 110, 111

photos, 81, 82, 83, 101, 106, 107, 108,
 109, 110, 111, 113, 211, 297, 347
police reports, 56, 57
pools and hot tubs, 80, 261
pre-approval, 198, 220
preparation time, 276, 301
previous bookings. *See* reservations,
 previous
price
 increases. See pricing, increasing
  your
 reductions. *See* pricing, lowering
  your
 tips, 90, 91, 92, 135, 136, 137, 138,
  139, 141, 142, 143, 144, 145, 165
pricing, 28, 75, 90, 91, 92, 133, 134,
 135, 136, 137, 138, 139, 141, 142,
 143, 144, 145, 146, 149, 152, 153,
 155, 156, 158, 160, 165, 211, 280,
 300, 336, 337, 347
 custom, 158, 159, 160, 226
 dynamic, 90, 135, 144
 fixed, 90, 91
 increasing your, 166, 167
 long-term, 164
 lowering your, 90, 91, 136, 138,
  155, 162, 167, 169, 170, 173,
  203, 211, 347
 monthly. *See* discounts, monthly
 weekly. *See* discounts, weekly
privacy, 64
private
 feedback. *See* reviews, private
  feedback
 messaging, 35, 218, 220, 225, 230,
  232, 235, 248, 308
 rooms, 76, 130, 332, 333
problems. *See* issues and problems
profile
 descriptions, 99, 100, 101
 photos, 85, 101, 102, 103, 194, 218,
  288
 videos, 103, 104
profiles. *See* Airbnb profiles
profitability, 19, 26, 27, 29, 32, 162,
 164, 172, 194, 196, 198, 231, 249,
 282, 323
property
 damage. *See* damage
 inspections, 30, 219

public
  feedback. *See* reviews, public
    feedback
  housing. *See* subsidized housing
  transport, 83, 115, 124, 125, 265,
    269, 295, 303, 304
push notifications, 203, 224, 229

R

rapport. *See* trust, credibility and
  rapport
ratings. *See* reviews and ratings
receipts, 56, 233
reciprocity, 130
red flags, 71, 230, 249, 251
references, 68, 70, 71, 291, 292
refunds, 184, 188, 189, 237
  fee, 184
regulations. *See* laws, legality, rules
  and regulations
reliability. *See* trust, credibility and
  rapport
rent controlled housing. *See*
  subsidized housing
rental real estate, 24, 28, 29
repairs. *See* maintenance, repairs and
  renovations
repeat stays, 244
reputation, 293
research. *See* independent research
reservation
  alterations, 238, 240, 241, 336
  requests, 68, 70, 72, 85, 94, 96, 97,
    98, 115, 126, 168, 173, 182, 194,
    199, 202, 203, 210, 219, 220,
    221, 222, 224, 225, 226, 229,
    230, 231, 280, 307, 318, 337
reservations, 60, 62, 74, 84, 87, 89, 90,
  91, 114, 136, 137, 169, 170, 181,
  182, 183, 188, 189, 190, 191, 197,
  198, 199, 203, 205, 210, 211, 214,
  215, 217, 218, 219, 220, 222, 224,
  226, 230, 232, 233, 238, 239, 303,
  317, 320, 330, 336, 337, 346, 347
  long-term, 62, 92, 162, 163, 164,
    170, 184, 215, 318, 321
  previous, 60, 87, 135, 210, 320
Resolution Center. *See* Airbnb
  Resolution Center

response
  rate, 194, 203, 224
  time, 224, 229, 337
responsiveness, 199, 201, 203, 210,
  229, 301
restaurants, 269, 295, 304
re-stocking supplies. *See* turnovers
revenue. *See* Airbnb, financial
  opportunity
review
  criteria, 248, 264, 295, 296, 298,
    300, 301, 303, 305, 344
  timeframes, 308, 309, 310, 311
reviews
  automated, 190
  giving, 307, 337
  negative, 70, 71, 204, 237, 255, 294,
    308, 311, 312
  positive, 40, 70, 71, 85, 91, 97, 155,
    200, 204, 210, 211, 214, 236,
    243, 244, 249, 258, 264, 274,
    277, 287, 293, 294, 295, 299,
    309, 311, 312, 344, 346
  primary, 200, 204
  private feedback, 306, 308
  public feedback, 306
  responding to, 190, 311, 312
reviews and ratings, 35, 68, 70, 71,
  190, 194, 200, 201, 204, 210, 211,
  214, 236, 243, 248, 274, 278, 287,
  293, 294, 295, 296, 298, 299, 300,
  301, 303, 305, 306, 307, 308, 309,
  310, 311, 312, 337, 344, 346, 347
room
  tax. See taxes, local
  type, 75, 192, 199
roommates, 32
Roomorama, 214
routing rules, 315, 317
rules. *See* laws, legality, rules and
  regulations
running a business. *See* business
  activity

S

safeguards and protections. *See* Airbnb
  safeguards and protections
safety amenities. *See* amenities,
  safety

trust, credibility and rapport, 33, 69, 98, 100, 101, 102, 103, 104, 128, 194, 212, 213, 214, 219, 234, 251, 263, 287, 288, 289, 290, 291, 293, 294
TurnKey Vacation Rentals, 214
turnovers, 87, 247, 276, 283, 284, 336, 337, 338
TV and media, 44, 261

U

under-pricing, 134, 136, 155, 162, 169, 211, 230

V

VacationRentals.com, 214, 319
valuables, 51, 59, 62, 63, 64
value, 204, 247, 258, 263, 264, 296, 305, 306
Value Added Tax (VAT), 31, 323, 329, 330

verifications, 288, 290
verified ID. *See* Airbnb verified ID
virtuous cycle, 40, 97, 194, 214, 249, 264, 294
VRBO, 89, 176, 214, 319

W

W.I.I.F.M. (What's In It For Me), 130
weather, 187
weekend pricing. *See* fees, weekend pricing
welcome notes. *See* notes, welcome
Western Union, 315
Whatsapp, 234
Wi-Fi. *See* internet and Wi-Fi
WIMDU, 214
workspaces, 200

Z

zoning codes and rules, 30, 31, 58, 94

Disclaimer

All information provided in this book is provided "as-is" and with no warranties. No express or implied warranties of any type, including for example implied warranties of merchantability or fitness for a particular purpose, are made with respect to the information, or any use of the information, within this book.

Whilst care has been taken to ensure that information contained in this book is true and correct at the time of publication, changes to Airbnb made after the time of publication may impact on the accuracy of this information. Evian Gutman gives no warranty or assurance, and makes no representation as to the accuracy, reliability or completeness of any information or advice contained in this book, or that it is suitable for your intended use.

Evian Gutman specifically disclaims liability for incidental or consequential damages and assumes or undertakes no responsibility or liability for any loss or damage suffered by any person as a result of the use, misuse or reliance of any of the information and content contained within this book.

If seeking further clarity on issues relating to Airbnb, both existing and prospective hosts should contact Airbnb or consult a lawyer or tax professional if they are unsure of anything.